THE LUXURY COLLECTION
EPICUREAN JOURNEYS

Content © Starwood Hotels & Resorts Worldwide
Design © 2014 Assouline Publishing
601 West 26th Street, 18th Floor
New York, NY 10001, USA
Tel: 212-989-6769 Fax: 212-647-0005
www.assouline.com
ISBN: 9781614281887
Printed in China.
Design: Jihyun Kim
Editor: Shoshana Thaler

THE LUXURY COLLECTION

EPICUREAN JOURNEYS

ASSOULINE

CONTENTS

INTRODUCTION
BY JOSHUA DAVID STEIN

Food often doesn't travel well. It bruises in transit or spoils en route. But the allure of food and the joy of mealtime travel excellently. It doesn't matter where one is. When it's half seven, the sun is two fingers from the horizon, and lunch is just a memory, dinner comes calling. These moments of pre-prandial anticipation are like Christmas Eve every night of the year. Wherever I find myself—Scottish moor, Balinese beach, the bustle of an Indian metropolis—suddenly the distance from home matters less than the distance to the table. Half the pull of the dinnertime bell is, of course, hunger. But the other half, the better half, is the promise of a good story. If one is lucky, a long evening of good stories. To sit at a table is to sit, spiderlike, at the nexus of a web of tales. At the best of tables some tales are told, some eaten, and all are consuming.

E. M. Forster once wrote, "Railway termini are our gates to the glorious and the unknown." If that's true, hotels are promised lands. To dine in a new city, deep into parts unknown, is to combine the histories of the kitchen and the culture, plus that agreeable frisson of a room full of like-minded travelers. Even the room itself, with neither food nor diners, can be magical. I remember the first time I ventured into the dining room of The Lambs Club, chef Geoffrey Zakarian's restaurant at the Chatwal Hotel on New York's 44th Street. It was moments before the inaugural dinner service; the tables were set but untouched. At that moment, just before the curtain opened, there were only a few black-clad servers silently brushing across the marble floor quickly and purposefully like a stage crew.

Even then, stories filled the air. The Lambs Club had been an actors' club, and from the wall, framed photographs of former club members like Charlie Chaplin and Douglas Fairbanks delivered their lines, too. The drama was intact. The crisp white linen tablecloth, pressed moments before, had character. Silly to call a tablecloth "quietly proud," but that's what it was. The spotless scarlet leather banquettes finished with shiny chrome end-pieces meters away from the worn 19th-century limestone fireplace, imported from a French château, bickered about whose grandeur was greater, the past's or present's. The details, like the delicate ridging of the crystal stemware that disappeared when the glasses were filled with water, told the story of craft; the custom-made salt-and-pepper shakers were tiny silver metaphors for love in the age of seasoning. Virginia Woolf wrote that one must have a room of one's own to write in, but rooms themselves can write, if one listens.

Eventually the curtains must rise, doors open and the restaurant comes alive. Tables do what they are meant to do: be laden. The restaurant is as a restaurant should be: filled with talk and laughter, the clatter of conviviality. Chairs are filled with hungry souls. Handsome, leather-bound menus are shown, and the meal begins. That first bite roots the diner, like a current running through him, to the ground. Even the most humble meals on familiar turf can do this, but especially while traveling, a shiftless state, this sense of groundedness is a lifeline. It's why one travels. Abroad, in terra incognita, it's a thrill. Each plate, when one chooses and eats well, contains an unknown, exciting history, edible vistas.

This volume is filled with recipes and culinary snapshots from the restaurants at the over eighty-five properties that constitute The Luxury Collection. After all, at their most successful, a hotelier and a chef have parallel passions. He or she must not only choose original ingredients of sterling quality, but treat them with respect. He must use technique to burnish, not obscure, their innate qualities. This is the hallmark of tremendous craftsmen, and it's shared among the chefs featured in this volume and the hotels, resorts, and spas in which they work. They till their homeland, harvest the heritage, and weave a compelling tale.

From the table in the courtyard patio of the Hotel Alfonso XIII's San Fernando restaurant, for instance, one sees the beautiful Sevillan sky stretching above you and the ornate Mudéjar arches lit up in the night. The hotel was built for the Ibero-American Exposition of 1929 and inaugurated by King Alfonso XIII on the occasion of his niece's wedding. What one sees—the painstakingly restored architecture, the ceramic tiles, called azulejos, glazed with pride—is relatively unchanged since Infanta Isabel's wedding night. One can almost hear the ornate royal toasts in high-flown Castilian.

But that's only part of the story. The presa Ibérica (roast free-range pork), accompanied by a Potato and Bacon Terrine (page 75), immediately whisks one to Jabugo, a tiny town approximately an hour and a half by car to the northeast of Seville, from where the famous ham is sourced. Jabugo is a town devoted almost exclusively to jamón ibérico, the rich, dark-red, nutty meat that's protected by the E.U. because it's so exceptional. The town square of Jabugo is la Plaza del Jamón; it's the mecca for pork. While one might not choose to travel to Jabugo, to be in Seville and not try jamón ibérico, specifically from Jabugo and preferably acorn-raised (called jamón ibérico de bellota), is to not be in Seville at all.

That sensation—the experience of a dish being somehow integral to your understanding of the destination—is repeated again and again as one travels through these pages. Halfway around the world, this instant localization is accomplished with radically different ingredients, as in the Gosht Qorma (page 29), an elaborately spiced lamb stew, at the ITC Mughal in Agra. Originally developed in the Mughal Empire, the stew has become an integral part of Uttar Pradesh's culinary culture. In Agra, the former capital, where the hotel occupies thirty-five manicured acres near the Taj Mahal, the connection between past and present isn't just made through the architecture or the silhouette of the Taj's mausoleum against the sunset, but also by tasting the same concatenation of spices as the sun sets half a millennium later over the same horizon.

The same, of course, can be said for the lobster roll (page 132) from The Equinox, on the banks of Vermont's Battenkill River. Taciturnity and lobster rolls are the twin keys to the New England psyche. And it's a measure of the range of human experience that that same lobster—now spiny—is made into Spaghetti with Lobster Ragù (page 94), an exuberant, outspoken dish, at the Hotel Cala di Volpe on Italy's Costa Smeralda in Northern Sardinia. It's as authentic an expression of the Sardinians' fiery temperament as the lobster roll's lemon-touched tartness is of the old New England fortitude.

In fact, nearly every recipe in this volume is accompanied with a piece of the culture from which it comes. The delicate interweaving of scallops, salmon roe, Chinese mushrooms, baby lobster, and silky tofu in the Twelve at Hengshan Hot and Sour Soup (page 34) is like mouthing the words to a conversation in a Shanghai bar. One may not understand the language, but viscerally, physically—after all, eating is a physical act— there's an exchange happening. The world is on a plate. Likewise, one can't prepare the hearty Halibut, Peas, and Pork Jowl recipe (page 92) from Turnberry Resort on Scotland's rugged west coast without feeling, at least a wee bit, the wind whipping up from the Irish Sea, if only in the immense comfort such a dish might provide a storm-battered Scot.

Of course, these are recipes meant to be prepared in one's home kitchen. They are meant either as a reminder of voyages past or a primer for voyages soon to be. The hope, of course, is to experience the food in situ. Even so, there's an adventure to be had in trying to find the patience dock so common in Ankara or the Bulgarian yogurt necessary for the Tarator, a cold cucumber soup (page 67) served at Sofia Hotel Balkan. (You can use cabbage and Greek yogurt, respectively, if you don't

succeed.) And, if one lives in New York City, half the fun of cooking anything from the Indian subcontinent is the trip to Kalustyan's, the spice emporium in Manhattan's Curry Hill.

One can use this book as a travel guide, without ever leaving one's home, but even more as a catalyst for journeys to come. One can only gaze at that Western Cowboy Burger (page 146)—epic tower of onion ring, pickles, and beef—for so long before one feels the need to visit Scottsdale's verdant oasis, The Phoenician, or look at the tender tiles of shrimp in the delectable and delicate Red Shrimp Carpaccio (page 59), chef Daniele Turco's signature dish at The Gritti Palace in Venice, before employing your own gondolier and crossing the ocean. These dishes are calls *en avant,* to sally forth, explore, and eat.

Food is the ultimate lens. And it is the reason so many of us journey on quixotic culinary quests. I've tooled across New Mexico in search of the perfect Green Chili Cheeseburger (Badlands Burgers in desolate Grants), through North Carolina looking for the best whole-hog barbecue (Skylight Inn, Ayden), and all over Paris for the perfect crêpe (in the shadow of the Gare Montparnasse at an old Breton crêperie called Ti Jos). And these journeys have never been about finding the ultimate thing or the place. The perfect steak frites, or the perfect anything really, is just a windmill to tilt after. But one meets great people along the way, food lovers both amateur and professionals, companions on one's culinary journey.

And if food attracts good people, it's also because it takes a good person to make great food. It takes skill, alchemy, mastery of craft, attention, and, importantly, relationships. That's the other story a perfectly prepared entrée tells. Behind every great chef is a great farmer or fisherman or forager. Beyond the battalion of the back of house—the *chef de cuisine, chef de partie,* down the line to the garde-manger and dishwasher—there's a company of men and women who do the literal work of harvesting what the ground, or water, offers.

So when one is in Paris enjoying chef Stéphanie Le Quellec's red mullets (page 64), it's not just a perfectly baked fish (the trick is in the livers!); one is actually tasting the fruit of chef Le Quellec's relationship with her purveyors, the fishermen and -women from Pas-de-Calais who cull the fish from the North Sea. It's the story of receiving the fish at ungodly hours, their eyes still shiny, gills red, and flesh still firm, chatting about the tempest swell of the sea that morning. In Mykonos, the scene is repeated at the fish market every morning, cries of "Γειά σου" traded between Stathis Thermos, the Santa Marina Resort's executive chef, and the superannuated, sun-beaten fishermen who pull from their blue crates sea bass, shimmering in the Mediterranean dawn.

Twelve hours later, that sea bass, sautéed and resting atop an aubergine salad, is on a plate at the BayView restaurant. Orkos Bay stretches into the darkness, lights are twinkling from the stacked-up houses on Mykonos's rugged coast. When one lifts one's gaze from the plate to the faces of those one dines with, when one imagines (if they don't actually appear as they so often do at the end of the meal) the noble visage of the chef—his crisp white jacket rolled at the sleeves, arms scarred from a life at the range—one needn't say a word for these stories to become a deafening and joyous hubbub. And after the petits fours are but crumbs, the Greek coffee drunk, and the ouzo glasses empty, when one goes off to dream or to journey deeper into the night, those stories don't end either. They just leave the table and travel alongside you. Bon voyage.

66 Food is the ultimate lens. And it is the reason so many of us journey on quixotic culinary quests. 99

STORY OF
THE LUXURY COLLECTION

The Luxury Collection is an ensemble of more than eighty-five of the world's finest hotels and resorts, each noteworthy for its architecture, art, furnishings, and cuisine. Our properties share a dedication to immaculate service and comfort, and each has a unique heritage that's inextricably tied to its location.

The collection has been curated for its unique spirit of diversity and genre; each Luxury Collection property has a story to tell. In this volume, you will find some of the singular stories that these hotels and resorts tell through their interpretations—traditional and creative—of the cuisines of their regions. As diverse a cultural ensemble as The Luxury Collection is, each hotel's careful attention to providing guests with an authentic and unique culinary experience binds them all.

Consider, for instance, Hot and Sour Soup at Hengshan Twelve, the buzzy restaurant in Shanghai's Twelve at Hengshan. As the urban-chic hotel blends the perfectly preserved Western Neoclassical and Art Deco elements of the Bund with modernized Chinese folklore, the chefs at Hengshan Twelve take the traditional dark brown soup of Shanghai and add the tender seafood of the south.

At the lavish Gritti Palace in Venice (home of some famous carpaccios), simple ingredients are elevated into works of art, such as a vibrant Red Shrimp Carpaccio with Ginger Gelato, tangy with citronette dressing (made, naturally, with olive oil from Lake Garda). At Al Maha, in Dubai, chefs look to ancient Egyptian history to create Um Ali ("Mother of Ali"), at Al Diwaan restaurant, combining indigenous camel's milk with pistachios, cashews, and Iranian saffron—a gently sweet custard (made with the not-so-strictly-traditional addition of Gewürztraminer raisins). In the Americas, Palacio del Inka showcases its locally sourced treasures, pairing quinoa (a global fad that began with the ancients) with Andean mushrooms in an elegant vegetarian plate. In North America, the traditional New England lobster roll is best served without deviation from tradition, as at The Equinox in historic Manchester Village, Vermont.

Throughout this volume, exceptional chefs of The Luxury Collection share their food memories, the ingredients integral to the cuisine of their region, and, most generously, the dishes that define their approach, so you can recreate your own food memories at home—or whet your appetite for a visit. Each of The Luxury Collection's properties offers the opportunity to meet a new destination in a completely unique way. We hope you will enjoy the stories—and the recipes—our collection offers.

THE LUXURY COLLECTION®

Hotels & Resorts

the NINES

AFRICA &
THE MIDDLE EAST

THE SHERATON KUWAIT
Kuwait City, Kuwait

TRIO OF KOFTA
WITH MUSHROOMS, MINT POTATO MASH, AND PLUM CHUTNEY

Serves 4

For the Plum Chutney:

14 oz fresh plums, halved and pitted

¾ cup plus 2 tablespoons oyster sauce

3 tablespoons cinnamon

1 oz ginger, chopped

4 cloves garlic, chopped

¾ oz finely chopped coriander

Salt and pepper, to taste

For the Chicken Kofta Skewers:

8 ½ oz ground chicken

4 blades lemongrass, for skewers

4 cloves garlic

⅙ oz red chili flakes

2 teaspoons oyster sauce

1 oz chopped cilantro

1 egg yolk

Salt and pepper, to taste

Olive oil, for cooking

This delectable recipe is made from ingredients that are indigenous to the Middle East.

- Make the chutney: Place all the ingredients in a pot over low heat; simmer, 30 minutes. Use a hand mixer to blend to a smooth consistency.

- Prepare the skewers: Combine the ingredients for the chicken kofta in one bowl, the beef in another, and the lamb in a third. Divide each into 4 portions, and skewer them on the lemongrass, forming the meat into long, cigarlike shapes on the skewers. Heat a little oil over medium heat and pan-fry the koftas until browned and well done.

- Prepare the za'atar: Wash it and cut it into 1 ½-inch-long pieces. Combine them with the mushroom quarters. Heat the olive oil in a frying pan and sauté the za'atar-mushroom mixture briefly. Season with salt and pepper to taste.

- Make the mashed potatoes: Cut the potatoes into pieces and boil until soft; drain. Combine with the cream and mint, season with salt and pepper, and blend until smooth and creamy.

- To serve, place a skewer of each type of meat on each of 4 plates, then put a dollop of chutney alongside them. Add some za'atar and mushrooms and garnish with the blackberries or raspberries. Form the potatoes into balls or dumpling shapes and place alongside.

For the Beef Kofta Skewers:

8 ½ oz ground beef tenderloin

4 blades lemongrass, for skewers

⅓ oz fresh ginger, chopped

⅓ oz fresh red chili, chopped

⅓ oz fresh green chili, chopped

4 cloves garlic, chopped

1 egg yolk

Salt and pepper, to taste

Olive oil, for cooking

For the Lamb Kofta Skewers:

8 ½ oz ground lamb loin

4 blades lemongrass, for skewers

16 cloves garlic, chopped

1 ½ oz rosemary, chopped

⅙ oz red chili flakes

1 egg yolk

Salt and pepper, to taste

Olive oil, for cooking

For the Za'atar Mushrooms:

14 oz fresh za'atar leaves

7 oz fresh mushrooms,
cut into quarters

2 tablespoons olive oil

Salt and pepper, to taste

Fresh berries, for garnish

For the Mint Mash:

5 ⅓ oz potatoes

¼ cup fresh cream

1 ¾ oz chopped fresh mint

Salt and pepper, to taste

THE SHERATON ADDIS
Addis Ababa, Ethiopia

HARLEQUIN OF RABBIT
AND BOUDIN NOIR WRAPPED IN PARMA HAM
WITH BROAD BEANS AND SWEET CORN SAUCE

Serves 4

For the Meat:

12 slices Parma ham

4 (5 ½-oz) rabbit loins,
each cut into 2 strips

Salt and pepper, to taste

4 (5 ½-oz) boudins noirs,
each cut into 2 strips

2 tablespoons olive oil

For the Corn Sauce:

1 tablespoon olive oil

1 small white onion, chopped

1 carrot, chopped

1 stalk celery, chopped

2 cloves garlic, halved

2 cups chicken stock

3 cups corn kernels

4 oz broad beans

Salt and pepper, to taste

For the Chive-Potato Hash:

3 oz smoked bacon, diced

4 teaspoons olive oil

2 potatoes, peeled and diced

Salt and pepper, to taste

1 tablespoon chopped chives

For the Cider Dressing:

1 cup apple cider

1 egg yolk

3 tablespoons finely chopped shallots

2 tablespoons cider vinegar

3 teaspoons Meaux mustard

Salt and pepper, to taste

⅓ cup olive oil

1 cup microgreens, such as
red and green shiso cress

1 cup pea tendrils

A roulade of black pudding and rabbit tenderloin enveloped in Parma ham, pan-roasted and served accompanied by a fine corn velouté, broad beans, chive-potato hash, and cider vinegar–moistened baby greens.

- Prepare the meat: Arrange 3 pieces of Parma ham side-by-side on a large piece of plastic wrap. Season the rabbit lightly. Arrange a strip of rabbit across the ham and a strip of boudin noir alongside. Lay another strip of boudin noir over the rabbit and a strip of rabbit over the boudin noir. Use the plastic wrap to roll the rabbit and boudin up tightly in the ham; secure the ends. Repeat with the remaining ham, rabbit, and boudin noir to make 4 roulades total. Chill for at least 8 hours.

- Make the sauce: Heat 1 tablespoon oil in a sauté pan and sauté the onion, carrot, celery, and garlic until soft. Add the stock. Bring to a boil, then turn down to a simmer. Simmer, uncovered, 45 minutes, adding more stock if necessary. Remove from heat and strain, discarding the solids. Add the corn; bring to a boil, then lower to a simmer, 15 minutes. Remove from the heat and cool slightly. Pour into a blender and blend at high speed until the sauce is very fine; then put through a fine-mesh sieve. Check the seasoning. Keep warm.

- Make the hash: Sauté the bacon in the oil. Add the potatoes and sauté until crisp and golden brown. Season with salt and pepper and toss with the chives. Keep warm.

- Meanwhile, make the dressing: Bring the cider to a boil in a saucepan. Cook until it's reduced to about ⅓ cup. Allow to cool completely. Transfer the cold reduced cider to a blender and add the egg yolk, shallots, vinegar, mustard, and seasonings. With the motor running, pour the oil in gradually in a slow, steady stream. Check the seasoning.

- Preheat the oven to 400°F. Heat 2 tablespoons olive oil until just smoking; add the meat roll and sauté until browned on all sides. Finish cooking in the oven, 15 minutes. Remove from the oven and allow to stand for at least 5 minutes before carving.

- To serve, mold the potatoes into the center of each plate. Carve each roulade into 4 pieces diagonally; arrange them around the potatoes. Toss the microgreens and pea tendrils in the dressing. Place the salad on top of the meat. Arrange the beans around the plate. Spoon the corn sauce over the beans, drawing the sauce across the plate in stripes.

WINE PAIRING
A light-bodied wine, such as a delicate Pinot Noir or a white Rhône-style wine.

AL MAHA
Dubai, United Arab Emirates

UM ALI

Serves 10

---

2 ¼ pounds breakfast
puff pastries

4 ¼ cups full-cream camel milk

Pinch Iranian saffron

8 large egg yolks,
lightly beaten

⅞ cup caster sugar

1 ¾ oz pistachios

1 ¾ oz cashews

1 ¾ oz Gewürztraminer raisins

1 cup whipped cream

Um Ali, or Mother of Ali, is a humble dessert and one of the most popular in the United Arab Emirates. It is the signature dessert dish of Al Diwan restaurant at Al Maha. Easy to prepare and suitable for any occasion, Um Ali has a perfect combination of sweet flavor and crunchy texture, to please even the most discerning palate.

- Preheat the oven to 375°F. Crush the pastries a little bit, then put them in the oven just until golden and crisp, about 10 minutes.

- Over very low heat, heat the camel milk with the saffron, egg yolks, and sugar, stirring constantly until thick enough to coat the back of the spoon, to make a basic crème Anglaise sauce.

- Take the pastries out of the oven, and pour the crème Anglaise on top. Mix them together, then add the nuts and raisins. Let the mixture rest for 1 hour or more.

- Scoop into ramekins, and place them in the oven for 5 to 10 minutes to heat through. Cover completely with whipped cream and serve immediately.

WINE PAIRING
This dessert pairs well with Special Late Harvest Orange Muscat & Flora, from Brown Brothers (Kings Valley, Victoria, Australia), with aromas of orange blossoms for the nose and fresh citrus for the palate.

GROSVENOR HOUSE
Dubai, United Arab Emirates

PESHAWARI SAMOSA
WITH CHAI ICE CREAM

Serves 12

For the Chai Ice Cream:

1 ¼ cups single cream,
or light cream

1 ¼ cups milk

6 tea bags

1 (½-inch) stem ginger,
peeled and crushed

½ teaspoon ground cinnamon

10 cloves

½ teaspoon fennel seeds

3 green cardamom pods

5 egg yolks

½ cup plus 2 tablespoons sugar

For the Samosas:

1 cup desiccated coconut

¾ oz ground almonds

¾ oz flaked almonds

¾ oz pistachios, chopped

¾ oz raisins, chopped

3 tablespoons plus 1 teaspoon
unsweetened condensed milk

1 ½ tablespoons granulated sugar

½ teaspoon ground cardamom

12 spring roll sheets

4 ¼ cups vegetable oil, for frying

1 ½ tablespoons all-purpose flour

Vegetable oil, for deep-frying

Dark chocolate, melted, for garnish

White chocolate, melted, for garnish

With this sweet interpretation, the samosa—India's most iconic dish—has evolved from its savory genre into a treat for the sweet tooth.

- Make the ice cream: In a pan bring the cream and milk to a boil. Remove from heat. Add the tea bags, crushed ginger, and spices. Set aside for 1 hour to allow the flavors to infuse.

- Strain the milk through a fine-mesh strainer.

- Whisk the eggs and sugar together until pale yellow in color. Stir this into the milk mixture and cook over low heat, stirring constantly until the milk thickens to a custard consistency or until it coats the back of a spoon. Let the custard cool to room temperature, then chill it in the refrigerator.

- Churn in an ice-cream maker according to manufacturer's directions. Reserve in the freezer until ready to use.

- Make the samosas: Combine the desiccated coconut, ground and flaked almonds, pistachios, raisins, condensed milk, sugar, and cardamom in a bowl; mix well to form the samosa filling. Divide into 12 portions.

- Cut the spring roll sheets into twelve 2-inch-by-6-inch rectangles and fold into samosa shells. Fill these with the samosa filling.

- Fill a pot with the vegetable oil and heat to 350°F. Deep-fry the samosas in batches until golden brown in color, setting on a towel to drain; set aside to cool.

- Place the melted dark chocolate and white chocolate in separate pastry bags fitted with thin tips. Place 1 samosa on each plate and garnish with dark and white melted chocolate piped in zigzag lines. Serve with a scoop of Chai Ice Cream.

THE OCEAN FIZZ

Serves 1

For the Hibiscus Agave:

1 cup water

1 cup light or amber agave

¼ cup hibiscus tea flowers

For the Ocean Fizz:

2 oz gin

4 ½ teaspoons hibiscus-infused agave (above)

4 ½ teaspoons freshly squeezed lemon juice

1 tablespoon pineapple purée

Ice

Splash of soda

Grated zest of lime, for garnish

In the great expanse of desert, there is an oasis where you can take in the breeze from the serene waters of the Arabian Sea and enjoy your first sip of an Ocean Fizz, a proprietary blend of gin, hibiscus-infused agave, fresh lemon, pineapple, a splash of soda, and a hint of lime.

- Make the Hibiscus Agave: Pour the water and agave into a pot; add the hibiscus tea flowers. Bring to a boil. Remove from heat and cover for 20 minutes. Strain out hibiscus flowers and let cool.

- Make the cocktail: Combine the gin, Hibiscus Agave, lemon juice, and pineapple purée in a shaker. Add ice and shake hard for 8 to 10 seconds. Add a splash of club soda and double-strain on ice into a Tom Collins glass. Garnish with lime zest.

ASIA

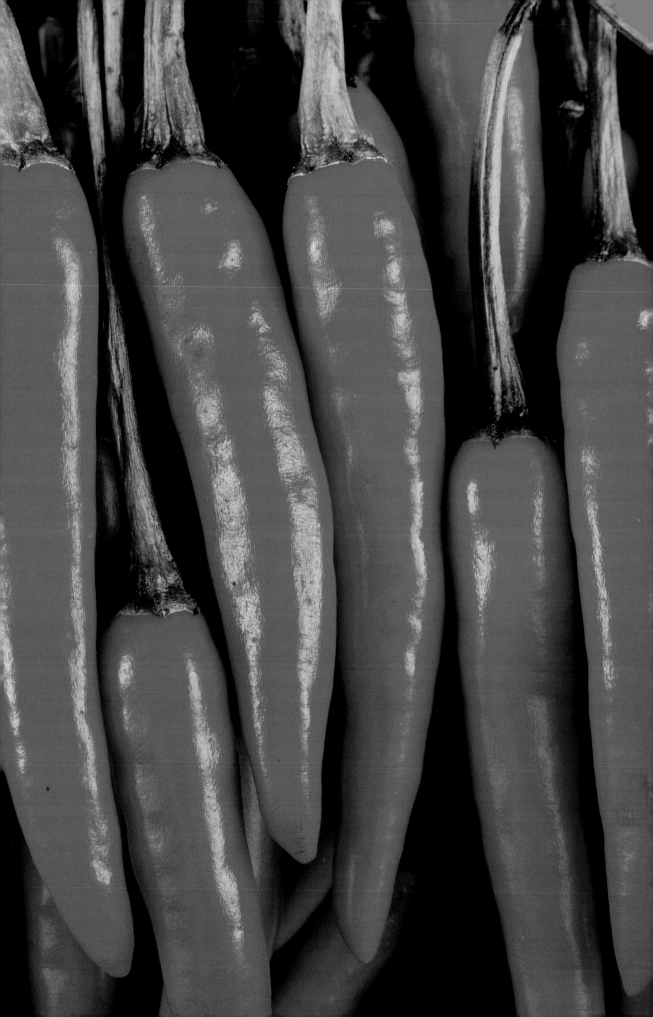

THE CASTLE HOTEL
Dalian, China

CHARCOAL-GRILLED WINTER OYSTERS
WITH GARLIC CONFIT AND DRIED CHILIS

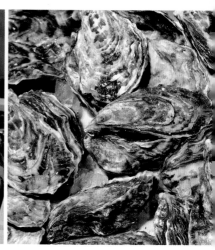

Serves 10

½ cup sugar

3 tablespoons rock salt

10 Dalian oysters (during winter)

About 20 medium cloves garlic

¾ cup plus 1 tablespoon milk

1 ¾ oz green chili, sliced

In Dalian, in Northeast China, the local people say, "Winter oyster, summer clam." As the sea gets colder, the oysters maintain enough fat for the long winter, making winter the ideal time for Dalians to harvest them. Bangchui Island, in the southwest of Dalian, produces oysters as big as a shoe, appropriately known as shoe oysters. This dish is a local favorite. The unique flavor of the Dalian winter oysters is enriched when they are cooked on a charcoal grill, and the garlic and chili enhance the flavor even more, making this dish one of the important local Dalian favorites.

- Preheat the oven to 125ºF. Spread the sugar and salt on a rimmed baking sheet with the chilis on top; bake 1 hour or until dried and crispy.

- Peel the garlic cloves and blanch; repeat 5 times using fresh water every time. Then boil the garlic in milk until simmering. Remove the garlic with a slotted spoon and put in a food processor or blender; process to a fine purée. Then pass it through a fine-mesh sieve.

- Preheat a grill. Clean the oysters, then put them on the grill until the shells open. Open each shell half, top with a spoonful of garlic confit, and garnish with the dried chilis.

WINE PAIRING
Local Dalian sea cucumber wine.

ITC GRAND CHOLA
Chennai, India

YETI GHEE ROAST

Serves 5

3 ½ oz whole byadgi chilis,
dry-roasted

2 tablespoons cumin seeds,
dry-roasted

10 cloves garlic,
peeled and crushed

¼ cup tamarind pulp,
diluted with ¼ cup water

1 tablespoon ground turmeric

2 ¼ pounds C-grade prawns,
peeled and deveined

Salt, to taste

⅔ cup ghee, or clarified butter

1 ⅓ cups thinly sliced red onions

Fresh cilantro leaves, for garnish

Wedges of lemon, for garnish

A Mangalorean delicacy, this dish is an innovative play on the classic Chicken Ghee Roast. Not for the faint-hearted, it is fiery red, tangy, and spicy. Do not skimp on the ghee, as it is the flavor of clarified butter that gives the dish its distinct flavor.

- Make a paste with the byadgi chili, cumin seeds, garlic, tamarind juice, and turmeric.

- Marinate the prawns with the above mixture and add a little salt. Allow to marinate for half an hour and refrigerate until required.

- Heat the ghee in a pan over medium heat, add the onions, and sauté until translucent.

- Add the marinated prawns and sauté along with the onion and cook until done.

- Serve hot, garnished with fresh cilantro and a lemon wedge.

WINE PAIRING
Conundrum Caymus Vineyard (California). This unusual wine is made with five grapes: Sauvignon Blanc, Muscat Canelli, Chardonnay, Semillon, and Viognier.

ITC MAURYA
New Delhi, India

SEEKH KEBAB

Serves 4
---

1 ⅓ pounds lean stewing lamb

1 teaspoon red chili powder

2 tablespoons grated ginger

8 cloves garlic

2 green chilis

Salt, to taste

2 teaspoons garam masala

1 ¼ oz grated cheddar cheese

10 sprigs cilantro

1 lemon, cut into wedges

World-famous Seekh Kebab, which comes from the northwest frontier of India, is known for its succulent, tender texture and burst of flavors. This lamb mince kebab is flavored with Indian spices and cooked over charcoal embers.

- Preheat a tandoor (clay) oven to 800°F or start up a charcoal grill. Pat the lamb pieces dry with paper towels.

- Put the lamb, chili powder, ginger, garlic, green chilis, salt, garam masala, and cheese in a food processor and pulse until meat is minced and ingredients are combined.

- Divide the meat mixture into 8 portions. Form each portion into a ball, then wrap each around a metal skewer; gradually spread the meat over the skewer so as to form a spindle shape with even thickness.

- If using an Indian clay oven, immediately place the skewers in the oven. If using a grill, place the skewers on the grill. Cook until meat is evenly browned on all sides, 4 to 5 minutes. Serve hot, with lemon wedges for sprinkling.

WINE PAIRING
Shiraz (Australia) complements the spicy, robust flavors of Seekh Kebab.

ITC MARATHA
Mumbai, India

BHARLELI VANGI

Serves 4

½ cup vegetable oil

8 cloves

5 teaspoons coriander seeds

8 black peppercorns

¾ cup sliced onion

1 ¾ cups grated coconut

1 teaspoon cayenne pepper

Salt, to taste

¼ teaspoon sugar

1 ½ teaspoons tamarind paste

1 cup chopped unsalted peanuts

¾ teaspoon turmeric

12 to 14 small eggplants

¼ cup finely chopped
cilantro leaves

Bharleli Vangi hails from the coastal region of Maharashtra in western India. Small brinjals (eggplants) stuffed with a sweet and spicy, peanut-flavored mixture draw out all the authentic flavors of Maharashtrian cooking. The eggplants have to be cooked over a slow flame with utmost care in order to preserve the flavors of this dish.

- Make the stuffing: Heat 2 tablespoons of the oil in a pan and add the cloves, coriander seeds, and peppercorns. Sauté for 1 minute. Now add the sliced onions and fry until brown. Add the coconut and stir-fry until browned; remove and allow to cool.

- Grind the mixture to a paste using a blender. Add a little water if needed. Add the cayenne, salt, sugar, tamarind paste, peanuts, and turmeric.

- Keeping the stem end intact, cut each eggplant lengthwise into quarters. Stuff the eggplants with this mixture.

- Heat the remaining oil in a pan over low heat, and add the stuffed eggplants. Cover the pan and cook on low heat, being careful not to let them burn (add a little water if necessary), until the eggplants are tender.

- Serve hot with roti.

WINE PAIRING
Any good "reserve" Cabernet Sauvignon to complement the sweet and spicy flavors of the eggplant.

ITC RAJPUTANA
Jaipur, India

SANGRI KI TIKKIYA

Serves 4

½ pound sangri, or haricots verts

½ pound potatoes, scrubbed

1 pound spinach

¼ cup mint leaves, finely chopped

2 green chilis, thinly sliced

¼ cup cilantro leaves,
finely chopped

Salt, to taste

1 teaspoon red chili powder

1 teaspoon garam masala
(available in most Indian stores)

Cornstarch, as needed

Unsalted butter, for cooking

Sangri is one of the most revered ingredients of Jaisalmer. These tropical Rajasthani desert beans are often showcased in Jaisalmer's rich cuisine. Here the sangri is combined with spinach to make flavorful tikkis or croquettes. The same dish is still quite resplendent when prepared with tender haricots verts.

- Soak the sangri for 1 hour in warm water, then boil for 10 minutes. Alternatively, if using haricots verts, cut the beans into small pieces and boil just until cooked, then plunge into ice water.

- Boil the potatoes, skins on, in a heavy, covered pan, until tender. Let them cool, peel them, then grate them.

- Blanch the spinach leaves in boiling water for 2 to 3 minutes; allow to cool. Drain the excess water and chop roughly.

- Combine the beans, potatoes, and spinach in a food processor. Add the mint leaves, sliced green chilis, chopped cilantro, salt, red chili powder, and garam masala, and pulse until well combined; add a little cornstarch if needed to bind the mixture. Divide into 4 equal portions. Form each into a ball, then flatten to make disks.

- On a heated griddle, melt some butter and grill the tikki, turning them occasionally, until they are crisp and evenly cooked on both sides.

WINE PAIRING
A medium-bodied fruity wine such as the Coonawarra Cabernet Sauvignon (Australia) would blend well with the sangri, whose subtle fruit texture along with the cilantro and green chilis complements the minerality of the Cabernet Sauvignon.

ITC MUGHAL

Agra, India

GOSHT QORMA

Serves 4

½ cup ghee, or clarified butter

4 green cardamom pods,
pounded lightly

2 black cardamom pods, pounded

2 cloves

1 tablespoon ginger paste

2 tablespoons garlic paste

2 cups finely sliced onions

1 ¾ pounds lamb shoulder, cut on
the bone into stew pieces

2 bay leaves

1 cup whisked yogurt

1 teaspoon red chili powder

1 tablespoon ground coriander

1 teaspoon ground
green cardamom

2 teaspoons ground mace

1 teaspoon freshly
ground black pepper

Salt, to taste

1 cup water

In this classic, quintessential stew from the Mughal period, lamb is slow-cooked in a smooth gravy, which is elegantly balanced with a plethora of spices. Over time this qorma has been refined further by the master chef in ITC Hotels' kitchens.

- Heat the ghee in a heavy-bottom pan on medium heat. Add pounded green and black cardamom and the cloves. Sauté until the spices start crackling and give off a pleasant aroma. Add the ginger and garlic pastes, sliced onions, bay leaves, and lamb stew cuts. Sauté the lamb continuously on medium-low heat until it browns and the clarified butter separates, about 30 minutes. Sprinkle a little water while sautéing as needed to make sure the lamb doesn't stick.

- When the lamb is almost cooked, add the yogurt, powdered spices, and salt. Continue stirring and sautéing until the clarified butter starts surfacing. Add 1 cup water, bring to a boil, cover, and let it cook on low heat until the clarified butter starts surfacing again and the lamb is well cooked.

- Serve hot, accompanied with Indian bread.

WINE PAIRING
Beaujolais Villages red wine (France).

ITC WINDSOR
Bengaluru, India

KADDU KA DALCHA

Serves 10

---

2 ¼ pounds chana dal
(Bengal gram lentils)

¾ cup ghee, or clarified butter

1 teaspoon mustard seeds

1 teaspoon cumin seeds

25 curry leaves

5 large red onions, sliced thin

1 teaspoon ginger-garlic paste

5 pounds bottle gourd,
peeled and cut into batons

3 teaspoons turmeric

2 teaspoons red chili powder

4 teaspoons ground coriander

Salt, to taste

7 oz (about 1 cup) tamarind pulp

2 teaspoons garam masala

A small bunch of cilantro leaves,
chopped, for garnish

A small bunch of mint leaves,
chopped, for garnish

Bengal gram lentils are paired with bottle gourd in a stew tempered with mustard and cumin. The sweetness of the lentils and bottle gourd is set off by the tanginess of tamarind. This dish is inspired by a famous dish from the court of Nawabs of Lucknow, where lentils were combined with lamb and stewed to perfection. In order to make it vegetarian, the recipe was tweaked by replacing lamb with bottle gourd.

- Boil the chana dal until tender, then mash them into a paste.

- Heat the ghee in a pan and add the mustard seeds, cumin seeds, and curry leaves. Add the sliced onion and sauté until golden brown. Add the ginger-garlic paste, bottle gourd batons, turmeric, chili powder, coriander, and salt. Cook well over low heat. Add the lentil paste, tamarind pulp, and 1 cup water, then bring to a boil.

- Lower the heat and simmer until soup reaches a thick consistency. Finish with garam masala and serve hot, garnished with chopped cilantro and mint.

WINE PAIRING
Robert Mondavi Pinot Noir (California) is a powerful wine with fresh aromas of wild blueberry and a hint of grenadine and black cherry, lending itself to the sour and spicy flavors of the dalcha.

KERATON AT THE PLAZA
Jakarta, Indonesia

SOPA AZTECA

Serves 6
---

3 oz large dried pasilla (negro) chili, stemmed and seeded

2 oz dried ancho chili, stemmed and seeded

2 oz dried mora chili, stemmed and seeded

3 tablespoons grapeseed oil

1 large Spanish onion, chopped

8 cloves garlic, peeled and finely chopped

2 vine-ripe tomatoes, chopped

3 quarts chicken broth (homemade is best)

5 1/3 oz fresh epazote, or dried (optional)

1 1/2 teaspoons salt, or to taste

4 teaspoons ground white pepper

1 pound boneless skinless chicken breast halves, cut into 1/2-inch cubes

1 large ripe Hass avocado, for garnish

7 oz queso Oaxaca, grated, for serving

2 to 3 oz totopos, or tortilla chips, for serving

1/2 cup jocoque, or sour cream, for serving

6 lime wedges, for serving

Though the name of this soup implies an Aztec origin, this version comes from the Tarascan people of Michoacán. Dozens of variations exist, often featuring a spicy tomato broth with different chilis as the garnish. One much-loved addition is chicharrón, or pork crackling, which works wonderfully well.

- Toast the chilis on a large, flat, dry skillet until nice and charred. Break them into small pieces.

- Heat the oil in a medium saucepan over medium-high heat. Add the onions and garlic and cook, stirring frequently, until golden brown (do not burn).

- Place the onions, garlic, tomatoes, and chilis in a blender; process until smooth.

- Heat a large pot over medium-high heat until hot. Add the purée and stir until thickened to a paste and the acidity of the tomatoes is gone, 5 to 6 minutes. Add the broth and optional epazote. Reduce the heat to medium-low and simmer, 15 minutes. Taste and season with salt.

- Add the diced chicken; simmer gently until the chicken is cooked through.

- Just before serving, cut the avocado flesh into small cubes. Pour the soup into bowls and garnish with the avocado. Serve with cheese, totopos, jocoque, and lime on the side.

WINE PAIRING
This dish is best paired with a dark Mexican beer such as Victoria. If you prefer wine, choose a dry white, such as Casillero del Diablo Chardonnay, 2010 (Chile).

TWELVE AT HENGSHAN
Shanghai, China

TWELVE AT HENGSHAN HOT AND SOUR SOUP
WITH LOBSTER AND SALMON FISH ROE

Serves 1
---

1 (³/₄-pound) live baby lobster

¹/₃ oz salmon roe

1 egg white

2 tablespoons potato flour

¹/₂ cup vegetable oil

1 tablespoon spicy soybean paste

³/₄ cup basic chicken stock

1 tablespoon Chinese cooking
wine (Shaoxing)

Ground white pepper, to taste

Sugar, to taste

Salt, to taste

¹/₃ oz bamboo shoot,
cut into thin strips

¹/₃ oz wood ear black fungus,
cut into thin strips

¹/₂ oz fresh scallop,
cut into thin strips

¹/₃ oz dried Chinese mushrooms

1 teaspoon silken soft tofu

2 tablespoons Zhejiang
black vinegar

In China, every region claims hot and sour soup as their own. In Shanghai, it is dark brown, filled with white pepper and dark vinegar. In Southern China, spicy fermented bean paste is used as a base, and it has a reddish hue. At the Hengshan Twelve Chinese restaurant, we use the Southern version, adding chunks of tender lobster to make a warming seafood soup.

- Place the lobster in an ice bath to put it to sleep. Using your hands, separate the body and tail by twisting and pulling them apart. Remove the lobster meat from the shells and cut into 1-inch pieces.

- Tear salmon roe into roughly 10 pieces. Rinse and pat dry with paper towels. Mix with egg white, then coat with about 1 tablespoon potato flour.

- Heat the oil in a wok over medium-high heat and deep-fry the roe until golden brown. Drain and set aside.

- Using the same oil, lightly deep-fry the lobster meat until cooked. Drain, leaving a little oil in the wok, and place the lobster in a serving bowl.

- Sauté the soybean paste in the wok until fragrant. Add the stock, cooking wine, pepper, sugar, and salt. Bring to a boil and add the bamboo shoot, wood ear fungus, scallop, dried mushrooms, and tofu. Mix the remaining potato flour with a little water to make a starch. Return the soup to a boil and thicken with potato flour mixture.

- Remove the soup from the heat, then add the vinegar.

- Pour the soup into serving bowls and top with fried squid roe. Serve immediately.

WINE PAIRING
Gaja Rossj-Bass Langhe Chardonnay with Sauvignon Blanc (Piedmont, Italy).

VANA BELLE
Koh Samui, Thailand

THAI BANANA BLOSSOM SALAD

Serves 2

For the Dressing:

1 ½ tablespoons dried shrimp

2 tablespoons tamarind concentrate

1 tablespoon freshly squeezed lime juice

2 tablespoons grated palm sugar

2 tablespoons fish sauce

1 tablespoon nam prik pao (chili paste)

¼ cup settled coconut cream
(do not shake the can; use the creamy
part that has settled to the bottom)

For the Thai Banana Blossom Salad:

2 banana blossoms

8 ½ cups water

Juice of 1 lemon

1 tablespoon salt

4 large tiger prawns, peeled with
tails intact, cleaned, cooked

3 spring onions, white part only,
thinly sliced

½ cup shredded fresh coconut

1 bunch cilantro, leaves picked

Dressing (above)

6 medium shallots, sliced and fried,
for garnish

This clean and crisp light salad, made from locally grown Southern Thai produce, combines fresh flavors and zingy tastes and is perfect for afternoon lunch.

- Make the dressing: Process the dried shrimp in a small food processor until finely chopped. Combine with the remaining ingredients.

- Make the salad: Remove the purplish-red outer bracts from the banana blossoms. Discard the flower-like clusters and thinly slice the inner bracts widthwise on the diagonal. Place these in a bowl filled with 8 ½ cups water, the lemon juice, and the salt, to prevent browning. Halve the banana blossom cores, slice them on the diagonal, and add to the acidulated water.

- Drain the banana blossoms and place them in a bowl. Add the prawns, spring onions, coconut, cilantro, and dressing, and toss gently to combine. Scatter with the fried shallots to serve.

WINE PAIRING
Stone Circle Chardonnay, 2010 (Australia).

THE LAGUNA
Nusa Dua, Bali, Indonesia

ZARZUELA

Serves 4
---

6 tablespoons olive oil

½ cup diced onions

4 cloves garlic, chopped

12 clams

7 tablespoons white wine

7 oz grouper or sea bass fillet

12 prawns

12 mussels

7 oz fresh squid, cleaned and
cut into rings

7 oz tomatoes, diced

7 oz red, green, and yellow
bell peppers, diced

2 cups chicken stock or water

Pinch of saffron

Cayenne pepper, to taste

Salt, to taste

Julienned zest of 1 lemon

3 ½ oz sliced almonds, toasted

Chopped basil

Chopped parsley

1 loaf baguette, sliced and toasted,
for garlic bread

Butter, for garlic bread

Chopped garlic, for garlic bread

Bali is blessed with an abundance of fresh seafood and herbs. In the expert hands of our talented chefs, these ingredients blend harmoniously to create zarzuela, the traditional Spanish seafood stew. Beautifully rich with succulent seafood and an aromatic broth, zarzuela is one of the signature dishes at Arwana, the beachfront restaurant at The Laguna, a Luxury Collection Resort & Spa in Nusa Dua, Bali. Serve it warm with toasted baguette smeared with butter and garlic for an appetizer or a complete meal.

- In a pan, sauté the onions and garlic in olive oil. Add the clams and white wine. Cook for 1 minute. Add the fish fillet, prawns, mussels, and squid. Cook for another minute.

- Add the diced tomatoes, bell peppers, chicken stock or water, and saffron. Let it simmer for 6 to 8 minutes. Add cayenne pepper and salt to taste.

- Sprinkle with the julienned lemon zest, almonds, and herbs.

- Serve with toasted baguette smeared with butter and chopped garlic.

WINE PAIRING
Hugel & Fils, Gewürztraminer, 2009 (Alsace, France).

SOPHIE DAHL

Model and author

66 Indonesia explodes with colors and tastes, and Bali brings together the best of that in one of the most beautiful and graceful places on earth. 99

WHAT IS YOUR FAVORITE DISH TO PREPARE?
I like slow-cooking stews and soups, things with a very definite beginning, middle, and end, which make the kitchen smell like a happy place to be.

WHAT IS YOUR MOST MEMORABLE MEAL?
My husband and I went to El Bulli just before it closed and had a ridiculously lovely meal. Brioche scented with rosewater, sea urchin roe, and edible chocolate cigars. It was sublime.

WHAT IS YOUR FAVORITE FOOD-WINE PAIRING?
Roast chicken with a good Mersault. Beer and New York pizza.

WHAT IS A DISH YOU CANNOT LIVE WITHOUT?
Scrambled eggs with chopped red chili, parsley, and grated cheese on rye bread. Kedgeree. I am obsessed with breakfast.

WHAT INGREDIENTS DEFINE BALI?
Fresh fish, coconut, and a surprising amount of meaty dishes, too. Spices, but never too heavy. Very fresh flavors.

WHAT ARE THE MOST POPULAR DISHES IN BALI?
My husband tried a more carnivorous dish called lawar at one of the more traditional nights at the hotel. It was meaty and coconutty, and he assured me it was delicious!

NO ONE SHOULD VISIT BALI WITHOUT EATING:
…or drinking the traditional Balinese brem drink—a sweet rice wine that is a wonderful digestif.

WHAT IS SPECIAL ABOUT THE CUISINE IN BALI?
Indonesia explodes with colors and tastes, and Bali brings together the best of that in one of the most beautiful and graceful places on earth. The Balinese are also some of the kindest and most hospitable people I have ever met.

THE ROYAL BEGONIA
Sanya, China

SEAFOOD PAELLA

Serves 4

2 garlic cloves, minced

½ cup fresh parsley, chopped

Pinch of saffron strands or
½ teaspoon powdered saffron

Coarse salt

1 cup olive oil

¾ cup chopped cured ham,
such as Serrano

4 oz chorizo sausage, sliced

12 ½ oz chicken, cut into small pieces

Salt and pepper, to taste

½ pound squid, cut into small pieces

½ pound halibut, cut into small pieces

½ pound swordfish, cut into small pieces

1 pound small or medium
shrimp, shelled

1 medium onion, chopped

2 tomatoes, peeled and chopped

1 green bell pepper, chopped

1 red bell pepper, chopped

½ pound cooked small clams,
in their shells

1 pound cooked mussels (reserve
a few shells for decoration)

3 cups short-grain rice

Juice of 1 lemon

3 cups hot fish broth

1 pound large crayfish

Parsley sprigs, for garnish

Lemon wedges, for garnish

Seafood Paella is an iconic Spanish dish. In Chinese culture, it shares the same reputation in Western cuisine as escargots and spaghetti. It originated 100 years ago in Valencia, the third biggest city in Spain. At that time there was no seafood in the paella, as seafood could not be kept for long periods. Rather, it was made of rice, chicken (or rabbit meat), and vegetables and is now called Paella Valenciana; it is a very beloved traditional dish in Valencia. Nowadays paella with seafood is the most popular version.

- In a small bowl or mortar, mash the garlic, parsley, saffron, and salt. Set aside.

- Heat the olive oil in a paella pan with a 15-inch base. Add the chopped ham and chorizo. Fry, stirring, for a few minutes. Remove to a warm platter. Sprinkle the chicken pieces with salt, add to the pan, and fry over high heat until golden on all sides. Remove to warm platter. Add the squid, halibut, and swordfish to the pan. Sprinkle with dash of salt and fry for two to three minutes until brown. Remove to a warm platter. Add the shrimp and sauté about 3 minutes, or until barely pink. Remove to warm platter. Add the chopped onion, tomatoes, and peppers. Sauté until soft. Return the cooked ham, chorizo, chicken, fish, and shrimp to the paella pan. Add the parsley-garlic mixture. Add the cooked clams and mussels, discarding any that have not opened.

- Stir in the rice and the lemon juice. Fry for 2 or 3 minutes. Pour the hot fish broth over the rice, stirring. Bring to a fast boil. Decorate with large crayfish around the edge of the paella pan. Simmer covered for 20 minutes, without stirring. Turn off the heat and shake the pan lightly to prevent the rice from sticking. Cover with a dry towel for 10 minutes (this allows rice to absorb any excess broth). Garnish with lemon wedges and parsley sprigs before serving.

WINE PAIRING
Columbia Crest Two Vines Chardonnay (Washington, USA).

THE HONGTA HOTEL
Shanghai, China

STEAMED YANGTZE SHAD FISH
WITH CHINESE RICE WINE

Serves 4

---

3 tablespoons plus 1 teaspoon
light soy sauce

½ cup plus 2 tablespoons
rice wine

5 tablespoons chicken stock

1 tablespoon sugar

1 teaspoon salt

1 whole (6 ½-pound) shad fish

10 ½ oz winter melon

1 oz dried ham, sliced

1 oz bamboo shoots

1 oz shiitake mushroom, sliced

1 ⅔ oz leek, cleaned and chopped

1 tablespoon sunflower oil

Steaming a whole fish is considered by many chefs to be one of the easiest and hardest things to do. The process is easy, yet few can master cooking the fish through to the bone without drying it. The secret to a great flavor is in the sauce, which must be prepared from scratch, and avoiding as much as possible incorporating too much of the fish's natural jus. In this classic Chinese preparation, the fish is topped with winter melon, ham, bamboo shoots, and mushrooms, then doused with hot oil, which releases the flavor of the aromatics into the flesh of the fish.

- Combine the soy sauce, rice wine, chicken stock, sugar, and salt to make the sauce.

- Cut the fish horizontally in half, clean and wash then place it in a steamer. Decorate the fish with the winter melon, ham, bamboo shoots, and mushrooms. Pour the sauce over the fish and steam for 10 to 12 minutes until cooked through.

- Add the chopped leek on top.

- Heat the sunflower oil in a small pan and pour it over the fish to make its skin sizzle.

- Serve immediately.

WINE PAIRING
The dish goes great with Chardonnay.

THE ASTOR HOTEL
Tianjin, China

CLASSIC GRILLED LOBSTER
WITH NIÇOISE VEGETABLES AND TARRAGON SABAYON

Serves 4
---

4 quail eggs

2 (2-pound) lobsters

8 tablespoons (1 stick) butter

1 ¾ oz long runner beans or green beans, blanched and refreshed in ice water

¼ to ½ pound new potatoes, skins on, cooked in salted water and diced in small cubes

1 oz black olives, halved

Salt and pepper, to taste

1 ¾ oz cherry tomatoes, cut into quarters

For the Sabayon:

3 tablespoons sour cream

2 egg yolks

1 tablespoon chopped fresh tarragon

Juice and grated zest of ½ lemon

Salt and pepper, to taste

The thirty-first president of the United States of America, Herbert Hoover, made the Astor Hotel his home when he first arrived in Tianjin in 1899. He even spent his honeymoon with his wife, Lou Henry Hoover, in the Astor Hotel, where he appreciated the many Western meals he ate there, particularly this grilled lobster dish.

- Preheat the oven to 300°F.

- Use a spoon to gently place the quail eggs in a pot of boiling water and boil for 4 minutes. Remove to a bowl of ice water to stop the cooking.

- Blanch the lobsters: Place a large pot filled with water over high heat. When the water comes to a boil, add the lobsters and blanch for about 2 minutes. Plunge into ice water to stop the cooking.

- Cut each lobster in half lengthwise, taking out the black digestive tract going along the tail. Remove the organs in the head cavity. Crack the claws and remove the claw meat; fill in the empty head cavity with the claw meat.

- Place the lobsters on a sheet pan and put them in the oven for about 5 minutes to gently warm.

- Remove the shells from the quail eggs and cut eggs into quarters.

- Put the butter in an ovenproof pan and add the beans, new potatoes, and black olives; season to taste and place in the oven to just warm through.

- Remove the vegetables from the oven and add the eggs and tomatoes. Place the lobsters on a platter or plates and top with the vegetables and eggs.

- Make the sabayon: Put the sour cream in a bowl and carefully whisk the egg yolks one by one into the cream. Add the tarragon and lemon zest, season to taste, and add the lemon juice little by little; be careful not to add it all at once, as the sabayon will break.

- Spoon the sabayon over the lobster and vegetables, and place in a hot oven or under a broiler to color. Serve hot.

THE SHERATON GRANDE SUKHUMVIT
Bangkok, Thailand

YAM SOM O GOONG
THAI POMELO SALAD WITH TIGER PRAWNS

Serves 4

For the Roasted Curry Dressing:

2 tablespoons palm sugar

1 tablespoon white sugar

1 tablespoon tamarind juice

3 tablespoons roasted curry paste
(nam prik pao)

2 teaspoons fish sauce

1 ½ tablespoons fresh lime juice

For the Pomelo Salad:

12 (20-ct) tiger prawns, shelled,
deveined, and poached just until
pink and firm to the touch

½ cup Roasted Curry Dressing
(above)

1 Thai pomelo, thick skin removed
and flesh flaked into small pieces

¼ cup chopped shallots,
fried until crispy

⅓ cup roasted coconut powder

½ cup cashew nuts, roasted
and roughly chopped

2 fresh kaffir lime leaves,
cut into a fine julienne

Salt, to taste

For the Garnish:

4 pieces fresh cha plu betel leaf

2 fresh kaffir lime leaves,
cut into a fine julienne

¼ cup chopped shallots,
fried until crispy

4 whole dried medium red chilis

4 (1-oz) pieces pumpkin, each
carved into a leaf shape

1 tablespoon fresh cilantro leaves

Chef Kesinee's exquisite Yam Som O Goong, or Pomelo Salad with Tiger Prawns, is a fresh and healthy dish bursting with flavor. The sweet flesh of the pomelo and poached tiger prawns are dressed with a blend of tamarind, lime, and roasted curry paste, and garnished with fried shallots, cashew nuts, cilantro, and fragrant kaffir lime leaves.

- Make the Roasted Curry Dressing: Place the palm sugar and white sugar in a small saucepan and melt over low heat. Remove from the heat and allow to cool slightly, then add the tamarind juice, roasted curry paste, fish sauce, and lime juice. Mix well.

- Make the Pomelo Salad: Place all ingredients for the Pomelo Salad in a stainless steel bowl. Mix well and adjust the seasoning.

- To serve, place one betel leaf on each of 4 serving plates. Arrange an equal amount of salad on each plate, then place 3 prawns per serving on top of the pomelo salad. Garnish with the julienned kaffir lime leaves, fried shallots, dried red chilis, carved pumpkin leaves, and fresh cilantro leaves. Serve immediately.

WINE PAIRING
Sileni Sauvignon Blanc (Marlborough, New Zealand).

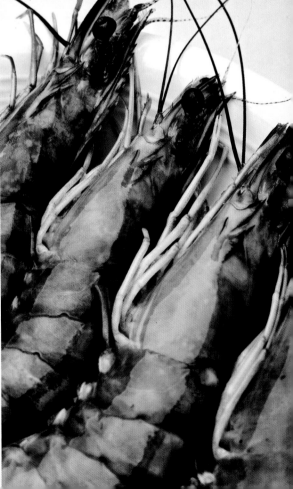

ITC GARDENIA
Bengaluru, India

PANDI CURRY

Serves 6
---

1 tablespoon coriander seeds

1 ½ teaspoons fenugreek seeds

1 tablespoon cumin seeds

1 tablespoon black peppercorns

3 medium onions, chopped

2 tablespoons chopped
peeled ginger

8 to 10 garlic cloves, chopped

2 ¾ pounds cubed boneless pork

1 tablespoon red chili powder

½ teaspoon turmeric

Salt, to taste

⅔ cup vegetable oil

1 cup water

1 tablespoon Coorg vinegar,
or malt vinegar

1 cilantro sprig

Pandi Curry has its roots in the Coorg region of Karnataka. Traditionally made with wild boar, it is flavored with a special vinegar called Coorg vinegar, made out of a wild black fruit known as kachampuli.

- Dry-roast the coriander seeds, fenugreek seeds, cumin seeds, and black peppercorns in a pan on a low flame until they turn dark brown.

- Make a paste of the onion, ginger, and garlic and set aside.

- Pat the pork cubes dry with paper towels and place in a bowl. Add in both the above mixtures and the red chili powder and turmeric, season with salt, and let marinate for about 1 hour.

- In a heavy-bottomed pot, heat the oil over medium-high, add the pork cubes, and sear until the sides of the cubes are sealed, stirring occasionally, 5 minutes. Add 1 cup water and cook on medium for 35 to 40 minutes, or until the pork cubes are tender.

- Remove from heat, let stand for a couple of minutes, then return to heat. Add the vinegar and cook for 3 minutes.

- Check for seasoning and remove to a serving dish. Serve garnished with cilantro sprig.

WINE PAIRING

Castello Banfi, Brunello di Montalcino (Sangiovese from Chianti), a wine leaving a rich to moderate taste of sour cherries with a snap of tartness, accompanies Pandi Curry very well.

ITC SONAR
Kolkata, India

BHAPA ILISH PATURI

Serves 4
---

1 ½ pounds hilsa fish,
cut into 4 darnes (steaks)

2 teaspoons salt

2 teaspoons turmeric

½ cup mustard paste

2 tablespoons lemon juice

5 green chilis,
seeded and chopped

4 large green banana leaves

Lemon wedges, for serving

The pride of Bengal, Bhapa Ilish Paturi is traditionally served at the Kali Puja festival that takes place during the ten days of Devi Durga celebrations.

- Season the fish with salt and turmeric and allow to rest for 15 minutes.

- Coat the fish evenly with the mustard paste. Sprinkle with lemon juice and chopped green chilis.

- Trim each banana leaf to make a 6-inch square, and wrap each piece of fish in a square; fold to resemble an envelope, and secure with cooking twine.

- Place the wrapped fish in a steamer. Steam the parcels for 10 to 12 minutes, or until the fish is cooked through.

- Serve each wrap garnished with a lemon wedge.

WINE PAIRING
Cabernet Sauvignon complements the fish's mustard flavors.

ITC GRAND CENTRAL
Mumbai, India

BAIDA PARATHA

Serves 8

For the Dough:

3 cups plus 3 tablespoons
whole wheat flour

1 cup plus 1 tablespoon
all-purpose flour

2 tablespoons vegetable oil

Salt, to taste

Water, as needed

For the Egg Mixture:

6 eggs

2 onions, chopped

½ inch ginger, peeled and chopped

2 teaspoons chopped cilantro

2 green chilis, chopped

1 teaspoon red chili powder

Salt, to taste

Vegetable oil as needed, for frying

Mint chutney, for serving

Baida Paratha is traditionally a breakfast specialty but has become a very popular street food in Mumbai.

- Make the dough: Combine the ingredients, adding water if necessary, to make a soft dough. Divide the dough into 8 pieces, then let it rest.

- Make the egg mixture: Break the eggs into a clean bowl. Add the chopped onions, ginger, cilantro, and green chilis. Add the red chili powder, and add salt to taste. Whisk the mixture to combine thoroughly.

- Season a frying pan with a small amount of vegetable oil and place over medium heat. Meanwhile, roll out the dough into thin round sheets.

- Cook a paratha until brown spots appear, then flip.

- Spread some egg mixture evenly on the paratha. Allow the mixture to cook. Once the egg is mostly cooked, fold in the edges to make a square shape. Flip the paratha and cook until the surface is evenly toasted. Repeat with the remaining dough and egg mixture.

- Serve hot along with mint chutney.

WINE PAIRING

Grenache-Mourvèdre-Shiraz blend (South Australia or Southern Rhône, France). The fruit-forward style and medium-bodied structure will complement the flavors and the body of the dish well, with the sweet-spicy notes of the wine adding an extra dimension on the palate.

CHEF MANJIT GILL

Corporate Chef, ITC Hotels

> **It is with care and emotions that you cook meaningful and soulful food.**

WHAT IS YOUR MOST MEMORABLE MEAL?

In 1988, I was privileged to partake in a meal cooked by an acquaintance at the Vanamali Ashram in Rishikesh, Geeta. The meal was entirely vegetarian, using only locally sourced produce, and cooked in the most pure and pristine way. Amazingly, Geeta used the entire vegetable in the preparation of the dishes she had cooked. In a dish made with beets, she included the beet stalks and its leaves. This meal changed my own approach to cooking.

WHAT IS THE MOST UNUSUAL THING YOU'VE EVER EATEN?

White turmeric, in both fresh and dehydrated forms, which is traditionally grown and sourced from the Deccan region in Southern India.

WHAT WAS YOUR FIRST COOKBOOK?

My mother! I learned many lessons: That the food prepared in your home—its flavor, taste, and variety—was not dependent on your socio-economic background but on the relevance of eating a meal with the family in your home. It is with care and emotions that you cook meaningful and soulful food. I now realize that this was my first lesson in managing food cost. My mother also taught me that taste supersedes tradition, techniques, and concepts.

WHAT IS YOUR FOOD OF CHOICE WHEN YOU WANT TO INDULGE?

Foods from the streets of India! Fresh, cooked on-site, flavorful, and tasty!

WHAT INGREDIENT DO YOU THINK PEOPLE SHY AWAY FROM, BUT SHOULD BE USED MORE?

Cold-pressed mustard oil.

WHAT INGREDIENTS DEFINE THE INDIAN SUBCONTINENT?

The subcontinent's wealth of spices and the innate knowledge of their uses; the variety of pulses indigenous to the region and the art of cooking them for wellness; the large number of staple cooking oils that are integrated into our daily cooking; the world's most fragrant rice, basmati, and the plethora of other rice varietals; the large repertoire of vegetarian dishes from every region in the country.

WHAT IS ITC HOTELS' PHILOSOPHY OF FOOD?

To present the "globe's best Indian cuisine and India's finest global cuisine." All ITC Hotels' culinary research and inventions are premised on this philosophy.

ITC KAKATIYA
Hyderabad, India

SHAHI TUKDA

Serves 4

¼ cup ghee, or clarified butter

4 thick slices whole wheat bread

6 ⅓ cups milk

¼ cup superfine sugar

1 teaspoon ground cardamom

Few strands saffron

¾ cup pistachios,
sliced into thin slivers

4 edible gold or silver leaves

Shahi (meaning "royal") Tukda (meaning "piece") is a dessert that certainly has many renditions. Eaten warm with an abundance of slivered pistachios or almonds, this dessert is comforting to say the least. The flourish of gold leaf adorning the mounds of patiently reduced milk, known as rabdi, is very pleasing.

- Heat the ghee or clarified butter in a skillet on a low flame. Once the ghee is hot, fry the sliced bread until it's golden brown and very crisp.

- In a heavy-bottom casserole, heat the milk just until it reaches the boiling point. Lower the flame and add the fried slices of bread, one at a time, into the simmering milk. Let them soak until the bread has absorbed the milk right into its core and softened. With a slotted spoon, lift the softened slices of bread and reserve.

- Add the sugar into the simmering milk and allow to cook until the milk reduces by half. Add the cardamom and the saffron and simmer for another 10 minutes, stirring occasionally to ensure the milk does not catch at the bottom of the pan.

- To serve, assemble the slices of bread on a plate, pour the reduced milk over the top, and serve garnished with pistachio slivers and gold or silver leaf.

WINE PAIRING
Viña Tarapacá (Chile). The acidity and dryness of this light-bodied wine complement the sweetness of the dish.

THE NAKA ISLAND
Phuket, Thailand

KHAO NIAW MAMUANG
MANGO AND STICKY RICE

Serves 4
---

1 cup Thai sweet or sticky rice

2 cups coconut milk

¼ cup palm sugar

2 teaspoons water

1 teaspoon cornstarch

2 ripe mangos

Toasted sesame seeds,
for garnish

Thailand's most famous dessert, Mango Sticky Rice is sweet, simple, and comforting.

- Soak the raw sticky rice in water overnight.

- Drain the rice and rinse it thoroughly. Then steam the rice for 20 minutes, or until tender.

- Place half of the coconut milk in a small saucepan. Warm over medium heat, stirring frequently, 5 minutes. Do not let the coconut milk boil.

- Pour enough warm coconut milk over the rice to coat it, then leave it to absorb, 15 minutes.

- Heat the remaining coconut milk in a saucepan over medium heat. Stir in the sugar. Simmer until sugar is dissolved.

- In a separate bowl, whisk together the water and the cornstarch. Whisk this into the coconut cream and cook over low heat for about 3 minutes, or until the mixture thickens.

- Slice the mango. Place the sticky rice on a plate and arrange mango slices on top. Drizzle with the coconut sauce, and sprinkle with a few toasted sesame seeds.

WINE PAIRING
For a sweet dessert like this one, we suggest Gewürztraminer Alois Lageder (Trentino Alto Adige, Italy). It has a full texture; low acidity; mango, peach, and apricot notes; and the spicy flavors of cinnamon and ginger.

THE ANDAMAN
Langkawi, Malaysia

STRAWBERRY REEF

Serves 10

For the Pickled Strawberries:
20 fresh strawberries
¼ cup raw sugar
Zest of 1 lemon, finely chopped

For the Candied Seaweed:
1 ³/₄ oz red and green seaweed
5 teaspoons sugar
1 tablespoon water

For the Coconut Ice Cream:
1 vanilla bean
1 ½ cups sugar
10 egg yolks
3 ²/₃ cups milk
1 ½ cups coconut cream
5 ½ oz dried coconut

This dessert represents the Andaman and its lovely surroundings. National Geographic has named the Andaman's beach the ninth best in the world, so we wanted to showcase the beach theme in a dessert. We made pistachio sponge cake to represent our corals, and tasty edible "sand" inspired by the unique sand at our resort. Served with fresh strawberries from Cameron Highlands and coconut ice cream made from young coconuts provided by our very own organic farmer, this makes a perfect ending to your dining experience!

- Prepare the pickled strawberries: Combine the strawberries, sugar, and lemon zest, and allow to marinate, 3 to 4 minutes.

- Make the seaweed: Bring a pot of water to a boil and blanch the seaweed for 10 minutes. Plunge into ice water, drain, then put in the refrigerator to chill. Repeat this process 3 times using fresh, unsalted water each time.

- Preheat the oven to 150°F. Melt the sugar with the water in a pan over high heat. Brush the seaweed with the sugared water and lay it out on a baking sheet. Place in the oven to dry until crispy, about 2 hours. Store in an airtight container.

- Make the ice cream: Scrape the seeds from the vanilla bean (reserve the pod) and place in a bowl with ¾ cup sugar and the egg yolks. Whisk until white and fluffy.

- Bring the milk, coconut cream, vanilla pod, and the remaining ¾ cup sugar to a boil; remove from heat.

For the Sugar-Glazed Pistachios:

1 tablespoon plus 2 teaspoons sugar

1 tablespoon water

1 3/4 oz shelled pistachios

3 tablespoons confectioners' sugar

For the Strawberry Purée:

7 oz frozen strawberries

2 tablespoons plus
2 teaspoons sugar

Juice of 1 lemon

For the Pistachio Sponge Cake:

2 3/4 oz shelled pistachios

1/2 cup sugar

1/4 cup plus 3 tablespoons
hot water

3 egg yolks

1/4 cup all-purpose flour

4 egg whites

1 2/3 tablespoons unsalted butter

For the Edible Sand:

2 3/4 oz butter cookies

1 3/4 oz waffle cones

1 oz toasted hazelnuts

4 teaspoons raw sugar

Dried coconut, for garnish

Mint leaf, for garnish

- Slowly pour a third of the milk mixture into the egg mixture, whisking rapidly. Slowly whisk the milk and egg mixture back into the pot with the rest of the milk mixture, and heat until it reaches 172°F, stirring constantly. Remove the vanilla pods and stir in the dried coconut. Pour into a plastic container and set in the freezer. Freeze, stirring every 15 minutes for a smooth ice cream, about 2 1/2 to 3 hours.

- Make the glazed pistachios: Melt the sugar with the water over low heat; remove from heat. Dunk the pistachios in the syrup to coat, setting the nuts on parchment paper to cool and dry. When they're dry, dust with confectioners' sugar.

- Make the strawberry purée: Place the strawberries in a pot with the sugar and a touch of water. Bring to a boil; remove from heat. Blend to a smooth and thick purée. Add the lemon juice. Place the purée in the refrigerator to chill.

- Make the cake: Toast the pistachios in a dry pan until fragrant. Add about 2 tablespoons of the sugar, and lightly shake the pan to move around the melting sugar. When the sugar starts to caramelize, add the hot water and cook for 5 minutes. Blend the mixture in a food processor and set aside.

- Whisk the egg yolks and the remaining sugar together until white and fluffy. Add the flour and the pistachio compound. In another bowl, beat the egg whites with a whisk or handheld electric beater until white and stiff. Fold it into the egg yolk mixture.

- Butter 10 microwave-safe ramekins and fill them halfway with the pistachio mixture. Bake in the microwave for 1 minute. Let cool in the ramekins for 2 minutes before removing and cutting in half.

- Make the edible sand: Place the cookies, waffle cones, and toasted hazelnuts in a food processor and blend until fine. Add the raw sugar and pulse to combine.

- To serve: Pour a spoonful of strawberry purée onto each chilled plate, and drag a line using the back of a spoon. Place the two halves of the pistachio sponge cake in the purée with the cut sides facing the middle of the plate. Place the glazed pistachios and pickled strawberries around the purée and cake. Arrange a few candied seaweeds around the sponge cake and a spoonful of edible sand between the cake halves. Place a scoop of ice cream on top of the sand and a bit of dried coconut on top of the ice cream. Garnish with a few mint leaves.

WINE PAIRING

Moscato d'Asti, Prosecco rosé, Kir Royale, or Sauternes.

EUROPE

CRAYFISH TARTAR
WITH ROASTED PEPPER MOUSSE AND BASIL

Serves 4

For the Crayfish:

12 crayfish

Zest and juice of 2 limes

1 chili pepper, chopped

½ oz ginger, peeled and grated

Chopped fresh cilantro

¾ teaspoon fleur de sel

Freshly ground pepper, to taste

4 teaspoons extra-virgin olive oil

For the Roasted Pepper Mousse:

2 red bell peppers

½ cup extra-virgin olive oil

2 tablespoons Xérès vinegar,
or sherry vinegar

2 tablespoons Dijon mustard

Salt and freshly ground pepper,
to taste

4 teaspoons basil oil, for garnish

Basil leaves, for garnish

A traditional Northern Greek recipe, from the village of Platamonas, at the foot of Mount Olympus. For the success of this dish, it is imperative that the crayfish is caught on the day it is to be served.

- Prepare the crayfish: Peel the crayfish and cut the flesh into small cubes. Add the lime zest and juice, the chili pepper, the grated ginger, the cilantro, salt, pepper, and olive oil. Mix to combine.

- For the Roasted Pepper Mousse: Using tongs, hold the bell peppers over an open flame until skins are wrinkled and charred. When cool enough to handle, remove the skin and seeds. Put the peppers in a blender and add the olive oil, vinegar, mustard, salt, and pepper.

- To serve, arrange the crayfish tartar and the roasted pepper mousse on each plate, topping with drops of basil oil and some basil leaves, for garnish.

WINE PAIRING
White Assyrtiko (Santorini Island, Greece).

THE PARK TOWER KNIGHTSBRIDGE
London, England

ROYAL KING CRAB RISOTTO
PARMESAN-EGG PANCAKES,
CANDIED TOMATOES, AND ARTISANAL SALAD

Serves 4

For the Candied Tomatoes:

4 large plum tomatoes

1 teaspoon olive oil

Salt and pepper, to taste

Pinch of sugar

1 clove garlic, sliced

Few sprigs lemon thyme

For the Parmesan-Egg Pancakes:

3 eggs

1 2/3 cups milk

1 teaspoon grated
Parmesan cheese

Salt and pepper, to taste

For the Crab Legs:

4 (3 1/2-oz) king crab legs

1 handful artisanal herb salad,
for serving

This combination is now one of our signature dishes, with a wonderful texture and sweetness from the crab.

▪ Make the candied tomatoes: Preheat the oven to 200°F. Bring a pot of water to a boil, then blanch the tomatoes, 6 to 8 seconds; remove them from the boiling water and plunge them into an ice-water bath. Remove the skins from the tomatoes. Cut them in half horizontally and remove all seeds.

▪ Put a sheet of parchment paper on a cooking tray and drizzle with olive oil; season the paper with salt, pepper, and sugar. Place the tomatoes on the tray, brush with olive oil, then season with salt, pepper, and a touch of sugar. Top each tomato half with a slice of garlic and some lemon thyme. Place the pan in the oven and cook for about 3 hours. They should be semi-dry, yet a little moist. Remove them from the cooking tray and keep them with their cooking juices in a small container until needed. These can be kept for up to 2 weeks in the refrigerator.

▪ Make the pancakes: Place the eggs, milk, and Parmesan in a bowl. Add a touch of salt and pepper and whisk well. Heat a nonstick pan over low heat. Spoon on enough batter to cover the bottom of the pan thinly, and cook slowly, just until it's cooked through, about 2 minutes; do not let it get brown. Use a spatula to gently remove the pancake to a plate lined with parchment paper. Repeat with the remaining batter.

Fresh lemon juice, to taste

Extra-virgin olive oil, to taste

A few shavings Parmesan cheese, for serving

A few shavings truffle (optional), for serving

For the Crab Foam:

2 tablespoons plus 2 teaspoons light crab broth, made from the crab body

7 tablespoons cold unsalted butter, cut into small dice

1 teaspoon black truffle oil

For the Beurre Noisette:

4 tablespoons unsalted butter

For the Risotto:

½ cup plus 2 tablespoons light crab broth

⅓ cup chicken stock

3 teaspoons olive oil

2 teaspoons chopped shallot

2 cloves garlic, chopped

¾ cup Arborio rice

2 tablespoons white wine

¼ cup grated Parmesan cheese

2 teaspoons heavy cream

½ teaspoon chopped truffle

Truffle oil

½ teaspoon chopped fresh parsley

½ teaspoon chopped fresh tarragon

- Prepare the crab legs: Cut the shell off each crab leg with scissors, being careful not to cut the meat. Remove the meat gently. Then cut each leg into 2 to 3 pieces and trim into neat cylinders, so they can stand on end. Reserve the trimmings to go in the risotto.

- Make the crab foam: Place the crab body in a pan and cover with water; bring it to a boil. Remove from heat and measure 2 tablespoons plus 2 teaspoons broth into a bowl, reserving the rest for the risotto. Add the butter and the truffle oil to the bowl of broth. Use a hand blender to blend it well until all the butter is dissolved and the sauce is light and frothy like a cappuccino. Keep warm until the risotto is cooked.

- Make a beurre noisette, or brown butter, by melting 4 tablespoons butter in a pan over low heat, cooking until it's bubbly and a nice golden color. Reserve in a small bowl.

- Make the risotto: Combine ½ cup plus 2 tablespoons of the crab broth you made in step 5 along with the chicken stock in a pot and bring it to a simmer. Heat the olive oil in another pot over medium-low heat. Add the chopped shallot and garlic, and just sweat them—do not let them brown—then add the rice. Stir the rice for 1 minute, coating it with the oil. Stir in the white wine and cook gently until the rice has absorbed all the wine. Add the warm stock and cook it gently for about 15 minutes. The risotto should be slightly flaky, with a slight crunch to it. When the risotto is cooked add the Parmesan, the cream, some chopped truffle, and a touch of truffle oil. Check the seasoning, and finish with the parsley and tarragon.

- Warm up the candied tomato, the crabmeat, and the pancake in the oven for 2 to 3 minutes or in the microwave for 15 to 20 seconds.

- To serve, place 2 candied tomatoes in the middle of each plate, then top with an egg pancake. Place 2 spoonfuls of risotto on half of each pancake. Fold the pancake over the risotto to form a half-moon shape. Set 2 pieces of crab on end next to it. Toss on a few leaves of artisanal salad, dressed with lemon juice and oil, to taste. Shave some Parmesan over the top, and a few shavings of truffle, if desired. Warm up the foam and blend it again; spoon some foam off and drizzle it on the plates. Finish with a few drops of beurre noisette.

WINE PAIRING
Paco & Lola Albariño 2011 (Rias Baixas, Spain). This native Spanish grape is known for its delicacy and roundness; its balanced minerals and acidity with its slightly sweet finish will complement this delicate dish.

JAMIE CULLUM

Singer, songwriter

66 My mum is a champion soup maker. She'll make a soup out of anything.... When I am home there is always something delicious bubbling on the stove. 99

WHAT IS YOUR FAVORITE DISH TO PREPARE?
The classic "man" dish: Sunday roast with all the trimmings—great robust dish that can feed 500. There is also something satisfying about making a fruit pie with fruit from the garden and homemade pastry.

WHAT IS YOUR MOST MEMORABLE MEAL?
My wife took me to eat at La Colombe d'Or, where we ate delicious French food under paintings donated by some of the former regulars, who just happened to be the likes of Matisse and Braque.

WHAT DISH REMINDS YOU OF HOME?
Any kind of soup. My mum is a champion soup maker. She'll make a soup out of anything. Hearty ham and pea soups, vegetable, chowders, chicken noodle—you name it. When I am home there is always something delicious bubbling on the stove.

WHAT IS YOUR FAVORITE FOOD-WINE PAIRING?
A quick-fried Dover sole and a nice Sancerre on a sunny veranda.

WHAT IS YOUR FAVORITE RESTAURANT IN LONDON?
It is hard to beat the River Café in Hammersmith. Some of the best food I've ever eaten in the whole world led by the food world's most beloved chefs.

HOW DOES THE REGION'S CULTURE CONNECT TO ITS FOOD/FLAVORS?
London is a melting pot of cultures. Its food history and current trends reflect that beautifully. Very much like the music that comes out of it as well. Ruthlessly modern, but underpinned by a sense of tradition and skill.

NO ONE SHOULD VISIT LONDON WITHOUT EATING:
Breakfast at The Wolseley is an institution!

THE GRITTI PALACE
Venice, Italy

RED SHRIMP CARPACCIO
WITH GINGER GELATO

Serves 4

For the Citronette Dressing:

½ cup extra-virgin olive oil from Lake Garda

2 ½ tablespoons freshly squeezed lemon juice

1 teaspoon Dijon mustard

Salt and pepper, to taste

For the Shrimp:

¾ cup finely diced zucchini

¾ cup finely diced cucumber

½ cup finely diced red bell pepper

½ cup finely diced celery

½ cup finely diced carrots

3 ½ tablespoons Citronette Dressing (above)

10 ½ oz red shrimp

Maldon salt, to taste

Freshly ground black pepper, to taste

2 tablespoons extra-virgin olive oil from Lake Garda

Watercress, for garnish

½ cup Ginger Gelato (below)

For the Ginger Gelato:

2 ¼ cups milk

1 cup plus 2 tablespoons heavy cream

1 vanilla bean

5 ⅓ oz ginger, peeled and sliced

5 egg yolks

½ cup sugar

The intention of this dish is to create a link between land and sea. All the ingredients are raw, enhancing their original characteristics. The extra-virgin olive oil used here is from the Veneto region. Its character blends beautifully with the fresh seafood and vegetables. The ginger ice cream that completes the dish balances it and gives it a fresh, slightly spicy note.

- Make the citronette: Whisk all the ingredients together well.

- Start the Red Shrimp Carpaccio: Combine the zucchini, cucumber, bell pepper, celery, and carrots, toss with the Citronette Dressing, and place in the refrigerator to marinate overnight.

- Make the Ginger Gelato: Mix all the ingredients and cook for 9 minutes in a Thermomix at 185°F, then freeze and Pacotize as needed. If the mixture is too grainy, add 2 to 3 tablespoons water and Pacotize again. Alternatively, cook the gelato over low heat, stirring frequently and being careful to scrape the bottom of the pan, until a temperature of 185°F is reached on a candy thermometer; remove from heat, strain, and cool to room temperature, whisking continuously over a bowl of ice. Place into the freezer. Remove the mixture when the edges start to freeze and churn vigorously with a fork, spoon, or electric hand mixer to break up the frozen parts. Place back into the freezer. Repeat this process 2–3 times until set.

- To serve, peel the shrimp, remove and discard the black vein, then slice them lengthwise very thinly. Arrange the marinated vegetables in a circle in the middle of each plate; dust the surface with a little salt and pepper. Arrange the slices of shrimp over the vegetables to form a spiral, and dress with olive oil, Maldon salt flakes, and freshly ground black pepper. Serve with a quenelle of ginger gelato and garnish with watercress.

WINE PAIRING
Alois Lagader Gewürztraminer (Alto Adige, Italy).

THE SHERATON ALGARVE
Albufeira, Portugal

PINE CLIFFS RESIDENCE
Albufeira, Portugal

TUNA TATAKI
WITH "XERÉM" OF CLAMS

Serves 4

For the "Xerém" of Clams:

2 ¼ pounds Portuguese clams

3 ½ oz smoked bacon, cut into thin strips

3 ½ oz chorizo, cut into small dice

3 ½ oz smoked ham, cut into small dice

7 tablespoons white wine

1 ¼ cups cornmeal, sifted

1 tablespoon salt

Freshly ground pepper, to taste

For the Bittersweet Fruits:

½ oz shallots, diced

1 to 2 cloves garlic, diced

3 ½ oz diced leeks

1 tablespoon olive oil

3 ⅓ oz vin jaune

1 cup fish broth

1 tablespoon safflower seeds

1 ¾ oz diced pineapple

1 ¾ oz sliced bananas

1 ¾ oz sliced papaya

7 tablespoons coconut milk

7 tablespoons heavy cream

1 tablespoon salt

For the Tuna "Tataki":

6 ½ oz sushi-grade ahi tuna

1 tablespoon flor de sal

½ tablespoon freshly ground black pepper

Juice of 1 lemon

1 tablespoon extra-virgin olive oil

This distinguished dish evokes the freshness of the products from the Algarve shoreline. It is prepared and presented by our young Algarvian head chef, Osvalde da Silva, who brings to the dish a touch of the local homemade flavor that has been passed down from generation to generation.

- Prepare the Xerém of Clams: Rinse the clams in a bowl with cold water. Cover them with salt water and soak, 4 to 5 hours.

- Prepare the fruits: Bring a pot of water to a boil and add the garlic, leeks, and shallots. Blanch just until soft, then drain.

- Heat the olive oil in a large sauté pan and add the blanched onions and garlic. Sauté until lightly brown and add the white wine. Pour in the fish stock and safflower seeds; add all the fruits. Simmer 5 to 10 minutes. Combine the coconut milk and the cream and add to pan. Season with salt.

- Prepare the tuna: Cut the tuna into 4 pieces, season with salt, pepper, and lemon juice, and stir-fry it in a sauté pan with the oil until lightly colored.

- Continue with the Xerém: Put a sauté pan over low heat and add the bacon, ham, and chorizo. Cook them until colored.

- Remove the clams from the water. Bring a pot of fresh water to a boil and add the clams; boil about 8 to 10 minutes. Drain the liquid through a fine sieve and reserve clams and liquid separately. Pour the liquid into a saucepan, add the wine, and bring to a simmer. Remove the pan from the heat, stir in the cornmeal. Bring back to boil then lower to a simmer, stirring occasionally, until thickened.

- To serve, divide the cornmeal mixture among 4 plates, top with the meat and clams.

WINE PAIRING
Alvarinho Soalheiro (Minho, Portugal).

HOTEL DES INDES
The Hague, Netherlands

MOLASSES-SEARED COQUILLES ST. JACQUES
WITH VEAL PASTRAMI AND SPICY APPLE JELLY

Serves 10

For the Spicy Apple Jelly:

2 cups sieved Goudreinet apple juice

1 red chili, seeded

1 teaspoon agar

3 sheets gelatin, soaked and drained according to package directions

For the Veal Pastrami:

¾ oz juniper berries

1 star anise

2 blades mace

4 bay leaves

⅓ oz caraway seeds

4 green cardamom pods

4 cloves

½ oz mustard seeds

1 tablespoon freshly ground black pepper

2 ¼ pounds rock salt

3 ½ oz muscovado sugar

2 ¼ pounds veal

For the Coquilles St. Jacques:

Muscovado sugar, crushed fine, for dredging

30 bay scallops

For Garnishes:

Chicory

Frisée salad with herbs

Apple blossom

Sliced Granny Smith apple

Extra-virgin olive oil

Crème fraîche

Molasses

Indulge yourself with a surprising combination of meat and fish, brought together with the spicy apple jelly.

■ Make the apple jelly: Bring the apple juice with the red chili to a boil. Lower the heat and simmer, 15 minutes. Strain, and pour back into the pot. Add the agar and bring to a boil again. Remove from heat and add the soaked gelatin. Let cool.

■ Line a rectangular platter with plastic wrap. Pour the apple jelly on the platter and place in the refrigerator.

■ Make the pastrami: Place everything but the veal in a food processor and pulse to combine. Roll the veal in the spice mixture, using only as much marinade as will stick to the meat.

■ Roll the meat tightly in plastic wrap, leaving both ends open so the moisture can drain out (place the wrapped meat in a dish to catch the juices). Place a heavy (flat) weight on top of the meat to flatten it, and place in the refrigerator to marinate, 12 hours.

■ Preheat the oven to 350°F. Place some wood chips in the bottom of a roasting pan and place the rack on top. Unwrap the veal and place it on the rack; place the roasting pan in the oven. Smoke the veal, 15 minutes.

■ Place the meat in a vacuum-sealed bag, place it in a Roner, and set to 130°F. Cook in the Roner for 3 hours.

■ Prepare the coquilles: Place the muscovado sugar in a bowl. Press each scallop in the sugar so one side is coated. Cook in a skillet over moderate heat until caramelized.

■ To serve, arrange 3 scallops on each plate in a triangle. Top with a little apple jelly, then a slice of pastrami. Garnish with chicory, frisée, apple, olive oil, crème fraîche, and a drizzle of molasses.

WINE PAIRING
Collovray & Terrier Domaine des Deux Roches Pouilly Fuissé Vieilles Vignes, 2011 (Maconnais, France).

LUGAL
Ankara, Turkey

STUFFED PATIENCE DOCK

Serves 4
---

2 bunches patience dock,
washed well, or cabbage

Salt and pepper, to taste

1 pound ground beef

4 tablespoons unsalted butter

2 onions, chopped fine

1 ⅓ cups bulgur or rice

½ bunch parsley, chopped

¼ bunch dill, chopped

⅓ oz dried mint

1 ½ tablespoons tomato paste

1 cup hot water

Yogurt, for serving

Minced garlic, to taste,
for serving (optional)

The capital city Ankara is one of the oldest developed areas in the Anatolian region. This area and its cuisine were influenced by different ancient civilizations. Efelek Dolması (Stuffed Patience Dock) is a reminder of this old era and is still a popular dish for modern Ankara and Central Anatolia.

- Place the patience dock leaves in salted boiled water for 5 minutes to soften them; plunge them into an ice-water bath to stop the cooking process.

- Brown the ground beef; remove from the pan. Melt 2 tablespoons of the butter in the same pan and sauté the onions until golden. Add the ground beef, season with salt and pepper, and cook, stirring, for 8 minutes. Add the bulgur to the onion-meat mixture and remove from heat. Let it cool. Add the chopped parsley, dill, and dried mint.

- Melt the tomato paste in 1 cup hot water.

- Place 1 leaf of patience dock on a clean surface, add 1 spoonful of meat filling; roll it up, closing the ends. Repeat with the remaining leaves and filling. Place all of the rolled patience dock in a pan side by side and season with salt. Pour the tomato sauce over the top and sprinkle with the remaining butter in pieces.

- Cover and cook over low heat, 20 minutes.

- Serve with yogurt mixed with minced garlic, if desired.

WINE PAIRING
This is an easy meal that will go with any wine, red or white
(you might try a Merlot).

PRINCE DE GALLES
Paris, France

RED MULLETS
WITH BOUILLABAISSE REDUCTION, GNOCCHI, AND BOTTARGA

Serves 4

For the Bouillabaisse:

1 onion, chopped

1 head garlic, cloves peeled and chopped

½ bulb fennel, chopped

Olive oil

3 tomatoes, chopped

2 ¼ pounds rockfish

1 oz tomato purée

3 tablespoons plus 1 teaspoon pastis

4 ½ cups water

Salt, to taste

Espelette pepper, to taste

For the Gnocchi:

1 pound rock salt

2 ¼ pounds russet potatoes

1 ⅓ cups all-purpose flour

Salt, to taste

2 egg yolks

For the Vichyssoise:

1 pound potatoes, peeled and cut into chunks

½ pound leeks, cleaned, trimmed, and sliced

½ cup olive oil

¼ cup vegetable stock

2 teaspoons unsalted butter

½ cup heavy cream

Salt, to taste

½ bunch of chives, chopped fine

For the Red Mullets:

8 (3 ½-oz) red mullets, scaled, slit lengthwise, boned, livers reserved

For the Garnish:

2 stalks of celery, brunoîsed (cut into tiny dice)

3 ½ oz bottarga, grated

5 leaves marjoram, for garnish

1 tablespoon heavy cream, for garnish

From a 100 percent Mediterranean catch, these red mullets surprise with their extreme freshness and release all the flavors of Provence with a hint of bouillabaisse and bottarga and the tender gnocchi.

- Make the bouillabaisse: Sauté the onions, garlic, and fennel in a little olive oil until soft. Add the chopped tomatoes, rockfish, tomato purée, pastis, and water and bring to a boil. Reduce heat to simmer until the bouillabaisse is no longer boiling. Season to taste with salt and Espelette pepper. Strain.

- Make the gnocchi: Preheat the oven to 350°F. Bake the potatoes on a ½-inch layer of rock salt on a rimmed baking sheet until tender, about 1 hour. Turn the oven down to 320°F.

- Peel the potatoes and press through a sieve. Combine with the flour, salt, and egg yolks. Mix together and form into 20 balls.

- Make the vichyssoise: Sauté the leeks and potatoes in olive oil until tender. Stir in the stock and the cream. Whip the vichyssoise to the consistency of whipped cream. Add a handful of chopped chives.

- Cook the red mullets: Crush the red mullet livers into a paste, and use a fork to spread them on the insides of the mullets. Cook the mullets upright, held together on a potato stand, 10 minutes.

- Meanwhile, just before serving, bring a pot of salted water to a boil and cook the gnocchi, in batches, until they rise to the top.

- To serve, spread 2 stripes of bouillabaisse on each plate, and place 2 mullets on top. Sprinkle both with celery. Place the gnocchi around the plate and sprinkle with grated bottarga. Add a leaf of marjoram on top of each gnocchi. Serve the vichyssoise cream on the side in a sauce dish. Put the remaining celery brunoîse in a small bowl, then add a swirl of cream on top, and sprinkle with more grated bottarga.

WINE PAIRING

Domaine La Préceptorie Cuvée Terres Nouvelles, 2011 (Côtes du Roussillon Villages, France).

STÉPHANIE LE QUELLEC

Executive Chef, Prince de Galles

66 More than a specific dish or place, the perfect meal to me is a warm moment you share with people you love, eating savory things, talking and laughing for hours. 99

WHAT IS YOUR FAVORITE DISH TO PREPARE?
Pot-au-feu, a traditional wintry French dish; it's a savory beef bouillon accompanying an array of meats and vegetables served with toasted pain Poilâne and marrow bones. Pot-au-feu is delicious with a lighter red—Sancerre rouge, Beaujolais Cru, or Bourgueil.

WHAT IS YOUR FAVORITE FOOD-WINE PAIRING?
A rib roast with a Vacqueyras, a red wine from Côtes du Rhône.

WHAT IS THE PERFECT MEAL?
More than a specific dish or place, the perfect meal to me is a warm moment you share with people you love, eating savory things, talking and laughing for hours.

WHAT WOULD YOU COOK FOR SOMEONE YOU JUST MET?
One of my signature dishes: calf sweetbreads cooked with prime girolle, mousseline of dates, lomito, and creamy Taleggio.

WHAT IS YOUR FAVORITE DISH IN PARIS, AND WHO MAKES IT THE BEST?
Brasserie-style dishes like the mimosa eggs at the restaurant Thoumieux.

WHAT IS PRINCE DE GALLES HOTEL'S PHILOSOPHY OF FOOD?
An authentic and generous cuisine that favors fine tastes and exceptional products. An accessible cuisine that seeks to provoke surprise and emotion through the simple yet elegant combination of flavors.

THE ROMANOS
Costa Navarino, Greece

OMEGA BEETROOT SOUP
WITH KATIKI CREAM CHEESE, GARLIC CHIPS, AND CITRUS FRUIT SALAD

Serves 4 to 6

For the Omega Beetroot Soup:

2/3 cup unsalted butter

1/3 cup chopped white onions

3 cloves garlic, chopped

1 carrot, chopped

1 leek, just the white part, cleaned and chopped

1 pound beets, peeled

5 cups chicken stock

1/2 cup freshly squeezed lemon juice

For the Katiki Cream Cheese:

2 teaspoons extra-virgin olive oil

1 clove garlic, finely chopped

2 3/4 oz katiki cheese

1/2 tablespoon chopped chives

1/2 tablespoon chopped lemon thyme

1/2 tablespoon chopped basil

1/8 oz Proti Island cream cheese

1 teaspoon freshly ground pepper

For the Garlic Chips:

1 clove garlic

3 1/2 tablespoons lowfat milk

1 tablespoon extra-virgin olive oil

1/2 teaspoon Proti Island salt

For the Citrus Fruit Salad:

1 pink grapefruit, peeled

1 lemon, peeled

1 orange, peeled

Extra-virgin olive oil, to taste

Fresh basil, chopped, to taste

The Romanos Resort takes the initiative on upscale and innovative dining, introducing the unique Omega concept through dishes that properly balance omega-3 and omega-6 fatty acids to boost the body's defenses against disease and help maintain healthy weight. This creative recipe by chef Doxis Bekris is based on the Omega Diet principles.

- Make the soup: Melt the butter in a pot over medium-low heat. Add the onions, garlic, carrot, and leek; sauté until soft. Add the beets; stir in the chicken stock little by little. Let it simmer until the beets get very soft. Remove from heat and add the lemon juice. Purée the soup and chill it immediately; season to taste.

- Make the cream cheese: Place the olive oil in a small pot over low heat and add the garlic. Simmer for 4 minutes, then let cool to room temperature. Strain the oil through a fine-mesh sieve, reserving the oil. Put the katiki cheese and the salt into a small bowl. Stir in the garlic-olive oil, herbs, and cream cheese. Refrigerate until ready to use.

- Make the garlic chips: Cut the garlic in half lengthwise and remove the green sprout. Thinly slice the garlic and put it and the milk in a saucepan. Bring the milk to a boil and remove from heat. Immediately strain out the garlic, reserving it; let cool. Put the olive oil in a pan over medium heat and add the garlic; fry the garlic until light brown and crispy. Remove the garlic from the olive oil and drain on paper towels.

- Make the fruit salad: Remove the fillets from the fruits and place them in a bowl. Add the olive oil and chopped basil.

- To serve, place a quenelle of Katiki Cream Cheese in each soup plate, top this with a spoonful of Citrus Fruit Salad and some Garlic Chips, then finish by pouring some Beetroot Soup around the salad.

WINE PAIRING
Whispering Angel Château d'Esclans Rosé, Grenache, and Syrah blend (Provence, France).

SOFIA HOTEL BALKAN
Sofia, Bulgaria

TARATOR
COLD CUCUMBER SOUP

Serves 1

1 cucumber, peeled, seeded, and cubed

5 to 6 cloves garlic, crushed

1 oz dill, finely chopped

5 to 6 tablespoons Bulgarian yogurt, or Greek-style yogurt

1 teaspoon sunflower oil, or extra-virgin olive oil

1 oz walnut pieces, ground

Salt, to taste

Tarator (Cucumber Soup) is a traditional Bulgarian dish. It is prepared mainly in the summer months, because it has a cooling effect, but many people enjoy it all year long. If you are far from Bulgaria and you want to taste again one of the traditional soups, favorite to all Bulgarians, you can make it on your own—it only takes a few minutes.

- Put the cucumber in a bowl; add the garlic, dill, and yogurt; stir to combine. Add enough water for a soupy consistency, as desired. Stir in the oil and walnuts. Add salt to taste.

CASTILLO HOTEL SON VIDA
Mallorca, Spain

GAZPACHO
OF APRICOTS, GREEN PESTO, AND AUBERGINES (EGGPLANT) IN TEMPURA

Serves 10

For the Gazpacho:

2 ¼ pounds ripe tomatoes

¼ of a green bell pepper

1 medium onion

9 oz ripe apricots, pitted

4 teaspoons extra-virgin olive oil

2 teaspoons white vinegar

Salt, to taste

For the Pesto:

17 oz fresh basil

5 oz pine nuts

2 cups extra-virgin olive oil

2 cups sunflower oil

7 oz grated Parmesan cheese

Salt, to taste

For the Aubergines in Tempura:

1 cup all-purpose flour

1 cup ice water

1 or 2 eggplants, depending
on size, about 5 oz

Vegetable oil, for frying

This is a typical summer dish and a variation of the traditional Spanish gazpacho.

- Make the Gazpacho: Cut the fruits and vegetables into pieces and process in a food processor until very smooth. Pass through a sieve.

- Make the pesto: Put all the ingredients in a food processor. Process until smooth.

- Make the Aubergines in Tempura: In a medium bowl, whisk the flour with the ice water until smooth (add some water if necessary). Cut the eggplant into sticks.

- Pour ½ inch oil into a pot and heat to 350°F. Dip the eggplant sticks in the batter and fry until golden and crisp, about 2 minutes. Drain on paper towels.

- To serve: Divide the gazpacho among 12 small glasses and top with the pesto. Add a fried aubergine stick and serve.

WINE PAIRING
Goes very well with a Chardonnay.

MYSTIQUE
Santorini, Greece

GREEK SALAD

Serves 4

¼ cup capers from Santorini

8 oz ripe tomatoes, sliced

2 ¾ oz cucumber, sliced

¼ green bell pepper, julienned

½ medium onion, julienned

2 ¾ oz feta cheese, cubed

2 ⅛ oz Kalamata olives

1 teaspoon fresh oregano

Sea salt, to taste

½ cup extra-virgin olive oil
from Kalamata

Greek food is a product of the country's hot climate and island makeup, but it relies on simple ingredients, making it easy to reproduce anywhere in the world. Among the basic staples of a Greek diet are vegetables, olive oil (used in most dishes), and feta cheese (a crumbly cheese made from goats' milk). When you mix them all together, the miracle of the Greek salad is revealed!

- Soak the capers in cold water for 15 minutes.

- Put the tomatoes and cucumbers in a deep dish. Layer the peppers and the onions on top, then the feta. Add the olives and the capers, then the oregano, sea salt, and olive oil.

WINE PAIRING
Fresh white Assyrtiko (Santorini).

HOTEL PRESIDENT WILSON
Geneva, Switzerland

WARM LOBSTER SALAD
CRUNCHY ROOTS IN HONEY-LEMON VINAIGRETTE, BARBAJUANS WITH CLAWS

Serves 4

For the Honey-Lemon Vinaigrette:
4 lemons, quartered
2 ½ tablespoons honey
¾ cup extra-virgin olive oil
4 teaspoons Xérès vinegar, or sherry vinegar
2 tablespoons Dijon mustard

For the Lobster:
1 carrot, chopped
1 onion, chopped
¼ leek leaf, chopped
¾ oz chopped thyme
1 bay leaf
1 stalk celery, chopped
2 cloves
Pepper, 3 pinches, or to taste
4 quarts plus 1 cup water
1 quart white wine
1 ⅓ cups white wine vinegar
Salt, to taste
4 (1-pound) lobsters

For the Root Salad:
4 mini red beets
4 mini yellow carrots, peeled and sliced very thin
4 mini orange carrots, peeled and sliced very thin
1 orange beet
1 ¾ oz salad shoots

For the Barbajuans:
1 ⅓ cups all-purpose flour
⅓ cup white wine
Pinch of lobster's coral
2 leaves of tarragon
Pinch of Espelette pepper
Pinch of salt
Groundnut oil, for frying

This is an easy gastronomic recipe with a touch of originality. The chef wanted to put forward a noble product, showcasing the lobster with simple vegetables.

- Make the Honey-Lemon Vinaigrette: Blanch the lemon quarters. Blanch again, for a total of 6 times. Add the honey, and let cook for 2 hours. Mix and let cool. Set aside ¼ cup plus 2 tablespoons of the lemon honey. Whisk the remaining lemon honey together with the olive oil, vinegar, and mustard.

- Prepare the lobster: Simmer the vegetables in the water, along with the wine and vinegar, 25 minutes. Season with salt.

- Add the lobster and simmer, 9 minutes. Remove the meat from the claws and tail; reserve the coral.

- Make the beet salad: Peel and slice the beets. Simmer them just until tender but still a bit crunchy. Let cool. Combine the vegetables with the lemon dressing.

- Make the barbajuans (ravioli) dough: Combine the flour, olive oil, lobster's coral, salt, and Espelette pepper. Roll the dough out to a thickness of 2mm. Divide it into 2 parts. On one part, place bits of lobster claw meat and tarragon. Place the other piece on top. Cut into squares around the filling to form the raviolis.

- Heat the oil to 350°F in a deep skillet. Fry the barbajuans until the dough is crispy and inflated, for less than 1 minute.

- To serve, brush the reserved lemon honey on each plate. Place 1 lobster tail per serving on the lemon honey, and top with the crunchy roots and salad shoots. Arrange the barbajuans on the side.

WINE PAIRING
Jean-Louis Mathieu Sauvignon Blanc (Chalais, Switzerland).

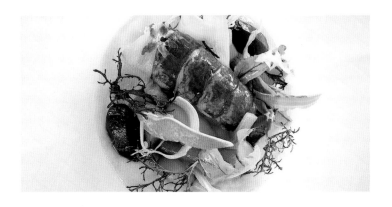

CONVENTO DO ESPINHEIRO
Évora, Portugal

TRADITIONAL ALENTEJO PORK FILLET
WITH ASPARAGUS MIGAS

Serves 4

For the Alentejo Pork:

6 cloves garlic, smashed

6 tablespoons paprika

4 bay leaves

Juice of 2 oranges

Pinch of salt and freshly ground black pepper

22 oz black pork fillet, sliced

5 tablespoons lard

5 tablespoons olive oil

4 oz black clams

¾ cup white wine

7 tablespoons chopped cilantro

For the Migas:

9 oz asparagus

3 cloves garlic, chopped

10 oz bread, torn into pieces

1 egg

Pinch of salt and freshly ground black pepper

The magic of Alentejo cuisine lies in its use of simple, indigenous products—olive oil made from Galega and Cordovil olives, meat from the Montado, Guadalupe bread, or the fresh herbs that grow spontaneously on the Alentejo plains—to create meals in which the pleasure of eating is like a cultural act.

- Prepare the pork: Combine 3 garlic cloves, the paprika, 2 bay leaves, the orange juice, and a pinch of salt and pepper. Rub this all over the pork and put in the refrigerator to marinate, 24 hours.

- Preheat the oven to 325°F. Heat the lard over medium-high heat in a frying pan; fry the pork in the hot lard until golden on all sides, then place it in a roasting pan. Roast for 10 minutes. Reserve the fat from frying the pork for the migas.

- In another frying pan, heat the olive oil and fry the rest of the garlic and bay leaves. Add the clams and the white wine and cover the pan. Leave for 5 minutes over low heat; discard any clams that have not opened. Add the cilantro.

- Make the migas: Boil the asparagus in salted water until tender; drain. Grind it in a food processor until smooth.

- Pour the fat from the meat into a skillet, and fry the chopped garlic in the fat; add the asparagus and then the bread pieces, seasoning with a pinch of salt and pepper. Stir until dry and add the egg (whole). Stir until the migas are loose.

- To serve, place 2 slices of pork on each plate with the migas on the side.

WINE PAIRING
2011 Rapariga da Quinta Tinto Riserva (Alentejo, Portugal).

HOTEL ALFONSO XIII
Seville, Spain

PRESA IBÉRICA
WITH POTATO AND BACON TERRINE

Serves 4

For the Potato Terrine:

¾ pound potatoes, sliced thin

7 tablespoons unsalted butter, melted

10 ½ oz bacon, sliced fine

6 ⅓ oz presa Ibérica (special cut of free-range Iberian pork)

1 ¾ oz smoked cheese, such as Idiazabal, grated

For the Sauce:

Dash olive oil

2 cloves garlic, chopped

1 shallot, chopped

1 wine glass of sherry

¾ cup beef stock

Salt and pepper, to taste

A handful of aromatic herbs, such as rosemary and thyme

The unique climate of the meadows of the region of Jabugo, Huelva, gives place to the best-quality products of Spain. This dish is a tribute to the farmers, who are so passionate about creating the best Spanish products, making Andalusian cuisine magnificent.

- For the Potato and Bacon Terrine: Preheat the oven to 250ºF. Line the base of a rectangular mold with a fine layer of potato slices followed by a drizzle of butter. Repeat the layers of potato and butter. Between every 6 layers, add a fine layer of bacon and sprinkle a handful of grated cheese, then continue layering potatoes and butter until the mold is full, placing a final layer of cheese and bacon on top. Bake for 2 hours.

- Remove from the oven and cool, placing a weight on top to ensure that the mixture remains compact.

- Start a grill and preheat the oven to 350ºF. Cut the terrine into 1-cm slices. Briefly place the slices on a grill to brown, and then bake for 2 minutes.

- Prepare the presa Ibérica: Clean and trim the meat, removing any excess fat. Cut into portions measuring 3 ½ inches by 1 ½ inches. Briefly place the meat on the grill to brown, then roast in the oven for 3 minutes.

- Make the sauce: Pour a dash of olive oil into a frying pan over medium heat and gently fry the garlic and the shallot. When they are golden, add the sherry and carefully flambé the mixture. Add the beef stock and bring to a boil. Lower the heat and simmer for 5 minutes. Season to taste with salt and pepper, then put the sauce through a sieve.

- To serve, place portions of the terrine on a plate. Slice the presa into escalopes and place on the plate. Coat with the sauce. Garnish with aromatic herbs.

WINE PAIRING

A red wine goes well with this dish—if possible, a Gratallops 2007 or a L'Ermita 2006 (both from Spain).

HOTEL DANIELI
Venice, Italy

THREE-COLORED RICOTTA GNOCCHI
WITH CUTTLEFISH, SEAFOOD, AND TOMATO AND BLACK CUTTLEFISH INK SAUCE

Serves 4

For the Gnocchi:

17 ½ oz ricotta cheese

Salt and pepper, to taste

3 ½ oz fresh pumpkin

About 5 medium potatoes, peeled

3 ½ oz beet, trimmed

3 ½ oz spinach

2 eggs

½ cup grated Parmesan cheese

1 teaspoon extra-virgin olive oil

Pinch of saffron

14 oz Italian 00 flour

14 oz potato starch

For the Seafood Sauce:

1 clove garlic

A handful of chopped parsley

Olive oil, for sautéing

17 ½ oz cuttlefish, diced

17 ½ oz San Marzano tomatoes, peeled and diced

A handful of chopped basil

2 ¼ pounds mussels, cleaned, opened, and removed from the shell

2 ¼ pounds venus clams, cleaned, opened, and removed from the shell

2 ¼ pounds razor clams, cleaned, opened, and removed from the shell

1 cup white wine

1 ¾ oz black squid ink

Chef Colucci's recipe takes inspiration from Maurice Prendergast's The Feast of the Redeemer *(ca. 1899). A riot of colors and textures blends together in this dish, representing the American artist's use of watercolors and pencil.*

- Start the gnocchi: Place the ricotta in a sieve, sprinkle a little salt on it, and leave it to drain overnight.

- The next day, preheat the oven to 350°F. Cut the pumpkin into chunks and sprinkle with salt. Wrap in a sealed packet of aluminum foil. Place on a baking sheet. Bake for 30 minutes, or until tender. Remove from the oven, and remove and discard the skin. Process the flesh to a fine purée in a blender or food processor.

- Boil the potatoes until tender. Drain and let cool. Mash, then put them through a sieve. Boil the beet in salted water until tender. When cool enough to handle, peel it, then purée it fine in a blender or food processor. Boil the spinach briefly, just until cooked. Drain, let cool, and process to a fine purée.

- Combine the eggs, potatoes, and drained ricotta; season with salt, a little pepper, Parmesan cheese, and the olive oil. Divide the mixture into 4 equal parts. Add the spinach purée to one part, the beet purée to another, the pumpkin to the third, and the saffron to the last part. Divide the flour and potato starch into 4 parts and add to each mixture. Mix to combine well.

- Put a pot of salted water over high heat to boil. With a rolling pin, roll out each ball of dough to a ⅓- to ½-inch thickness; cut these into strips and roll into a snake form. Cut each snake into small pieces and roll these into balls in a sieve to give them a little texture.

- Cook the gnocchi in batches in the boiling water, removing them as they rise to the surface. Set aside.

- Make the seafood sauce: In a large pot, sauté a garlic clove and a little parsley in olive oil. Add the mussels, venus clams, razor clams, and the white wine. Cook for a few minutes, just until the shells open. Remove the shellfish and strain the broth. Place the strained broth and the shellfish back into the pot, along with the diced cuttlefish, tomatoes, basil, and the remaining parsley. Bring to a light boil. Add the gnocchi, toss to coat, and heat through.

- To serve, place a small circle of squid ink on each serving plate and, with a wooden skewer, draw small lines out of the circle. Arrange the gnocchi on the plates and serve.

WINE PAIRING
Livio Felluga Sharis Chardonnay, Ribolla Gialla (Italy).

HELENA CHRISTENSEN

Model, photographer, philanthropist

WHERE DID YOU LEARN TO COOK? OR WHO/WHAT INSPIRED YOU TO START COOKING?
My mother inspired me; she's Peruvian, and all of my childhood I would be with her in the kitchen while she cooked all these delicious meals. Our house was always filled with the scent of spices and herbs.

WHAT IS YOUR FONDEST MEMORY OF/WITH FOOD?
Finding our own oysters off the side of the cliffs on a riverside in Australia. I really enjoy eating food straight from nature!

WHAT DISH REMINDS YOU OF HOME?
Smorgasbord, very Scandinavian.

WHAT IS YOUR FAVORITE FOOD-WINE PAIRING?
Chilled Sancerre with burrata and tomato salad.

WHAT IS A DISH YOU CANNOT LIVE WITHOUT?
My mother's chili con carne.

WHAT IS YOUR FAVORITE DISH IN ITALY, AND WHO MAKES IT THE BEST?
Pasta with white truffles, best served in Bice.

NO ONE SHOULD VISIT ITALY WITHOUT EATING:
Freshly caught fish in one of the little seaside towns.

WHAT IS SPECIAL ABOUT THE CUISINE IN ITALY?
I love the freshness of the ingredients, along with the comforting feeling of the pasta dishes with a bunch of Parmesan on top.

> **"I really enjoy eating food straight from nature!"**

BLUE PALACE
Crete, Greece

DUSKY GROUPER WITH OKRA

Serves 6

---

4 ½ pounds okra,
trimmed and chopped

2 pounds tomatoes, chopped

2 medium onions, chopped

4 cloves garlic, chopped

1 bay leaf

7 tablespoons white wine

1 bunch parsley, chopped

4 ½ pounds dusky grouper,
scaled and cleaned

Sea salt or table salt and freshly
ground black pepper, to taste

Juice of 2 lemons

1 ¾ cups extra-virgin olive oil

This two-hundred-year-old dish combines all the ingredients that made the diet of Crete famous: fresh fish, sun-grown vegetables, extra-virgin olive oil, and wine.

- Preheat the oven to 350°F.

- Combine the okra, tomatoes, onions, garlic, bay leaf, wine, and parsley in a bowl.

- Place the whole fish on a rimmed baking sheet and sprinkle with salt, pepper, and lemon juice. Arrange the vegetable mixture around the fish, and sprinkle the olive oil all over the fish and the vegetables. Place the tray in the oven and bake for 2 hours and 30 minutes.

WINE PAIRING
Enjoy this spectacular dish with a Greek Chardonnay or a Sauvignon Blanc. Alternatively, you can try a rosé wine made from Kotsifali and Mantilaria from Crete.

HOTEL FUERSTENHOF
Leipzig, Germany

GRILLED FILLET OF VEAL
WITH POLENTA TARTLET AND MIXED BEANS

Serves 6

For the Polenta:

1 3/4 cups chicken stock

3/4 cup polenta

1 stick unsalted butter

1 cup grated Parmesan cheese

Salt and pepper, to taste

Pinch of sugar, or to taste

2 eggs, beaten

Olive oil, for frying

For the Veal:

Olive oil, for frying

1 (2-pound) fillet of veal,
cut into 6 portions

Salt and pepper, to taste

2 branches fresh rosemary,
chopped fine

3 tablespoons unsalted butter

2 cloves garlic, chopped

1 shallot, chopped

14 oz mixed green beans

Pinch of sugar, or to taste

"Creativity and handiwork" is the favorite credo of Chef de Cuisine Till Weiss and his team. As the Italian and French way of savoring exquisite cuisine is loved by both domestic and international gourmets, Till Weiss inspires himself and his team to interpret classic modern dishes in the Mediterranean style.

- Preheat the oven to 325ºF.

- Make the polenta: Bring the chicken stock to a boil and sprinkle in the polenta. Lower to a simmer and cook for about 5 minutes, stirring constantly. Add the butter and Parmesan, and season with salt, pepper, and sugar to taste. Stir in the eggs.

- Spread the polenta in a 1-inch layer on a plate and let it cool down. Cut the cold polenta into 6 equal portions. Heat a skillet over medium heat and add a little olive oil. Fry the polenta until golden brown and keep warm.

- Prepare the veal: Heat a little oil in a large ovenproof sauté pan. Season the veal all over with salt and pepper. Brown the veal fillets gently, then place the pan in the oven. Bake until a meat thermometer registers 133°F for rare. Remove from the oven and place over medium heat. Add the rosemary, 2 tablespoons butter, and half the garlic. Once the butter starts sizzling, turn the veal to coat and glaze the meat, 1 minute. Remove the veal to a warm plate and let it rest 1 minute before slicing.

- Melt 1 tablespoon butter in a sauté pan and sweat the shallot and the remaining garlic until soft (don't let them brown). Add the beans and season with salt, pepper, and sugar to your liking.

- Serve slices of veal along with the polenta tartlet and beans.

WINE PAIRING
Böhme Vineyard Cabernet Dorsa and Cabernet Dorio, 2009 Cuvée (Saale-Unstrut, Germany).

HB

HOTEL BRISTOL
Warsaw, Poland

YOUNG POLISH DUCK BREAST SOUS-VIDE
MARINATED WITH BISON GRASS

Serves 4

---

1 pound 12 oz duck breast

Salt and freshly ground pepper, to taste

2 to 3 stalks bison grass (also known as sweet grass, buffalo grass, holy grass), crushed

2 ¼ oz Polish bison grass vodka (Żubrówka)

7 oz carrots

7 tablespoons unsalted butter

½ vanilla bean, seeds scraped and reserved

6 tablespoons plus 2 teaspoons coconut milk

1 tablespoon sugar

1 large Granny Smith apple, peeled and sliced

4 teaspoons apple juice

¾ cup plus 1 tablespoon duck demi-glace

Traditional Polish bison grass vodka matches perfectly with duck meat, giving it a unique and original taste.

- Score the skin on the duck gently with a sharp knife. Season the meat with salt, pepper, and crushed bison grass. Sprinkle with a little of the bison grass vodka; close everything in a vacuum bag, and place in the refrigerator to marinate, 12 hours.

- Slice the carrots thin. Place them in a pot over low heat with 3 tablespoons of the butter and the vanilla seeds, and stew until the carrots are tender.

- Add the coconut milk to the carrots and season with salt and pepper. Place in a food processor and pulse to combine.

- Caramelize the sugar in a frying pan then add the apple slices; cook until lightly caramelized. Add the apple juice and 2 tablespoons butter.

- Cook duck sous-vide at 136°F in a circulator for about 45 minutes. Remove the bag from the circulator and let the meat rest for 8 minutes, so that it absorbs the juices.

- Bring the demi-glace to a boil and add the Żubrówka vodka; remove from heat. Slowly whisk in the remaining 2 tablespoons butter to give the sauce a velvety texture.

- Place a sauté pan over medium-high heat until very hot. Remove the duck breast from the bag and place it, skin side down, on the pan just until the skin gets crispy. Slice the breast into thin pieces.

- Place the apples on a platter, then top with duck slices and a splash of carrot mousse. Finish with duck demi-glace flavored with bison grass vodka.

WINE PAIRING
Fritz Allendorf Quercus Pinot Noir, 2008 (Rheingau, Germany).

HOTEL MARIA CRISTINA
San Sebastián, Spain

HAKE WITH AJOBLANCO

Serves 4

For the Hake:

4 tablespoons salted butter,
plus a little more for grilling

²/₃ teaspoon truffle oil

Freshly ground black pepper, to taste

1 ³/₄ pounds hake,
cut into 4 equal portions

For the Ajoblanco:

23 oz almond paste

4 ¼ cups water

2 ½ teaspoons olive oil

1 teaspoon sherry vinegar

1 teaspoon minced garlic

Salt, to taste

Truffle oil, for garnish

Microgreens, for garnish

Ajoblanco is a popular Spanish cold soup typical of Andalucia, in the south. It is believed that its origin dates back to the Roman times. Normally made with grapes or melon, this popular version from the north of Spain calls for hake, and the Ajoblanco is used more as a sauce than a soup.

- Prepare the hake: Melt 4 tablespoons butter in a saucepan over low heat and add the truffle oil and pepper.

- Make the Ajoblanco: Put the almond paste in a Thermomix, food processor, or blender and add the water, olive oil, sherry vinegar, garlic, and salt. Set at high speed and mix until all ingredients are well blended, at least 15 minutes. Remove and pass through a fine sieve. Keep in the refrigerator until ready to use.

- Start a grill. Spread a little butter on the hake and grill it to an internal temperature of 160ºF, 6 to 7 minutes, flipping halfway through.

- Warm the Ajoblanco gently, without letting it boil. Pour the soup into 4 bowls, place the hake on top. To finish, drizzle a little truffle oil over the dish. Garnish with sprouts.

WINE PAIRING
Marqués de Riscal Sauvignon Blanc or Limousin (Rueda, Spain).

HOTEL PULITZER
Amsterdam, The Netherlands

GRILLED DRY-AGED WEIDERUND RIB-EYE
CARROTS, NEW POTATOES, & BÉARNAISE SAUCE

Serves 4

For the Gastrique:

2 shallots, chopped

1 ²/₃ cups white wine

½ cup plus 2 tablespoons vinegar

1 ³/₄ oz tarragon, chopped

10 peppercorns, crushed

¼ tablespoon salt

For the Carrots:

1 yellow carrot, peeled and sliced

1 red carrot, peeled and sliced

1 purple carrot, peeled and sliced

3 tablespoons unsalted butter

2 sprigs rosemary

For the New Potatoes:

4 large new potatoes

Sea salt, to taste

1 clove garlic, chopped

Olive oil

For the Béarnaise Sauce:

2 egg yolks

1 ¼ cups (2 ½ sticks) unsalted butter

Tarragon, finely chopped

Salt and pepper, to taste

½ cup gastrique (above)

For the Steak:

4 (6-ounce) dry-aged rib-eye steaks

Discover the round taste of an aged delicacy combined with old-time favorites: carrots and potatoes, and a classic Béarnaise sauce.

- Preheat the oven to 375°F and start a grill.

- Make the gastrique: Place the shallots, wine, vinegar, tarragon, peppercorns, and salt in a pot and bring to a boil. Reduce heat and simmer until reduced to a quarter of its volume.

- Cook the carrots: Simmer each color carrot separate from the others in water with 1 tablespoon butter, rosemary, and salt until just cooked through, about 4 minutes. Drain.

- Cook the potatoes: Cut the potatoes into ¾-inch-thick slices. Use the rim of a cup to shape them into perfect circles. Boil the potatoes in water with salt and garlic, 5 minutes. Drain the potatoes and let them dry. Place them in a pan, toss with a little oil, and bake the potatoes until golden brown, about 5 minutes, flipping them halfway through. Sprinkle with sea salt. Reduce the oven temperature to 350°F.

- Make the Béarnaise sauce: Put the 2 egg yolks, ½ cup of the gastrique, salt, and pepper into the top of a double boiler. Whisk until the eggs reach about 60°F and are nice and creamy. Just before the mixture looks like scrambled eggs, whisk in the melted butter for a creamy sauce; add the tarragon.

- Grill the rib-eye: Grill the steaks, flipping, just until black grill marks are visible on each side. Sprinkle with salt and pepper. Place the steaks on a pan and cook in the oven for 4 minutes. Just before serving, put the steaks on the grill once more to heat through. Slice each steak.

- To serve, place each sliced steak on a plate. Arrange the potatoes and carrots alongside it and drizzle Béarnaise sauce around it.

WINE PAIRING
Château de Lisennes, Merlot-Cabernet Sauvignon-Cabernet Franc (France).

ARION RESORT & SPA
Athens, Greece

FILLET OF RED MULLET
WITH STUFFED COURGETTE FLOWERS

Serves 4
---

4 spring onions, chopped

4 cloves garlic, chopped

Extra-virgin olive oil, for frying

2 green bell peppers, chopped

8 ½ oz split peas

¾ cup white wine

¾ cup seafood broth

Salt and pepper, to taste

8 mint leaves, chopped

Grated zest of 1 bitter orange

⅔ cup sunflower oil

All-purpose flour, for dusting

8 courgette (zucchini) flowers

8 red mullet fillets

7 oz stamnagathi (spiny chicory) greens, chopped

2 oz fresh dill, chopped

Arion Resort & Spa, with its breathtaking view of the Aegean Sea, invites you to enjoy this tasty Mediterranean seafood recipe: a flavorful dish of fried red mullet fillet served with stuffed courgette flowers.

- Sauté ⅔ of the chopped onions and the chopped garlic in a little olive oil until soft. Add the chopped pepper and the split peas and stir once. Add the wine and the seafood broth. Add salt and pepper and bring to a boil. Reduce to a simmer and cook until the peas are just tender—be careful not to let them get too soft. Remove from the heat and add the chopped mint and bitter orange zest. Allow to cool.

- Heat the sunflower oil in a pan over medium heat. Place the flour in a shallow dish; add salt to taste. Stuff the courgette flowers with the pea mixture, coat the flowers in the flour, and fry in the sunflower oil until browned and cooked through.

- Fry the mullet fillets in some olive oil over medium heat until browned but still juicy.

- Sauté the greens with the remaining chopped onion until soft, then add the dill.

- To serve, place the stamnagathi in a shallow bowl, put the mullet fillets on top, and arrange the stuffed courgette flowers on the side.

WINE PAIRING
Amethystos Sauvignon Blanc–Semillon-Assyrtiko (Greece).

66 We must promote local products and people should support them in their cooking! This is how we will advertise ourselves, by word of mouth.... 99

STRATOS KALATHAKIS
Executive Chef, Arion Resort & Spa

HOTEL IMPERIAL
Vienna, Austria

SAUTÉED SADDLE OF VENISON
JUNIPER BERRY JUICE, WITH CABBAGE AND GRAY POPPY SEED ROULADE

Serves 4

For the Cabbage:

2 teaspoons red wine

2 tablespoons sugar

1 pound sweet cherries

Juice of 1 lemon

4 teaspoons sweet cherry juice

5 juniper berries

1 teaspoon caraway

½ cinnamon stick

1 bay leaf

1 ¾ pounds white cabbage, cut into thin strips

For the Potato Dough:

3 tablespoons unsalted butter, plus more to spread on pastry

½ cup milk

⅔ cup all-purpose flour

1 egg

Austria has a long history of game hunting, and in autumn the butcher shops and high-end supermarkets abound with game. This recipe brings the distinct yet delicate taste of venison to life— and you into the festive spirit.

- Prepare the cabbage: Purée the red wine, sugar, sweet cherries, lemon, and sweet cherry juice in a blender. Place the juniper berries, caraway seeds, cinnamon stick, and bay leaf in a spice bag. Place the cabbage, spice bag, and cherry mixture in the refrigerator and marinate for at least 24 hours.

- Cook the cabbage in the marinade, along with the spice bag, over low heat until it's soft, about 35 minutes.

- Make the dough for the Poppy Seed Roulade: Preheat the oven to 300°F. Bring the butter, milk, and salt briefly to a boil. Remove from heat. Stir in the flour until the dough is smooth; the dough should form a ball, detaching from the pot. Stir in the egg. Allow to cool.

- Boil the potatoes until tender. Drain and let cool. Put the potatoes through a sieve, then stir together with the dough.

- Make the filling: Sauté the speck briefly and drain in a strainer. Sauté the onions in the fat from the speck until golden brown. Douse with white wine, and let it boil down. Add the chopped parsley. Thicken with breadcrumbs and poppy seeds. Season with salt and pepper. Add the chopped garlic and then stir the drained speck and the egg into the mixture.

1 pound russet potatoes,
peeled and cut into chunks

Nutmeg, to taste

Salt and pepper, to taste

For the Poppy Seed Filling:

3 1/2 oz speck, chopped
into thin strips

1 medium onion, chopped fine

4 teaspoons white wine

3/4 oz parsley, chopped

1 3/4 cups breadcrumbs

3/4 cup gray poppy seeds

Salt and pepper, to taste

1 clove garlic, chopped fine

1 egg, beaten

For the Roulade:

2 puff pastry sheets, thawed

Unsalted butter

For the Venison Chops:

2 1/4 pounds saddle of venison,
with bones

8 juniper berries, crushed

4 sprigs thyme, leaves stripped
and chopped

Olive oil, for frying

1 onion, sliced

1 carrot, chopped

1/4 celery root, chopped

1 teaspoon tomato purée

1 cup red wine

2 cups beef consommé

1 bay leaf

3 peppercorns

1 tablespoon cranberries

1 tablespoon unsalted butter

- Roll out one sheet of puff pastry; spread with butter and lay the other sheet on top. Spread the potato mixture on the puff pastry, followed by the poppy seed pulp. Starting on a long side, roll up the pastry. Set the roulade in a baking dish, place the dish in a water bath, and steam in the oven for 45 minutes.

- Prepare the venison: Trim the fat from the saddle of venison (reserving the trimmings) and cut into 4 chops. Rub the chops with 4 crushed juniper berries and the thyme; let sit for about 60 minutes.

- Fry the venison trimmings lightly in the oil together with the onion slices, the carrots, celery root, and tomato purée until brown. Deglaze with the red wine, then add the beef consommé, bay leaf, the remaining 4 juniper berries, the peppercorns, and the cranberries, and let it boil for about 20 minutes. Pour through a strainer and boil down until reduced to a thick, velvety texture.

- Turn the oven heat up to 325°F. Season the chops with salt and pepper. Heat a little olive oil in a large ovenproof pan over medium-high heat and sear the chops. Add some butter to the pan, and bake in the oven for 10 minutes until just pink inside. Take the chops out of the pan and cook briefly in the same pan with the game sauce.

- To serve, arrange the cabbage on each plate and place a chop alongside it; pour the sauce around the venison. Serve extra sauce in a sauce boat.

WINE PAIRING

A single-vineyard Blaufränkisch (red wine from the Austrian province of Burgenland) or a full-bodied Merlot.

HOTEL NATIONAL
Moscow, Russia

TENDER BRAISED GOAT
IN CANNONAU WINE WITH OLIVE OIL, WHIPPED POTATOES, AND TOMATO TARTAR

Serves 8

For the Braised Goat:

5 ½ pounds goat meat, bone-in

Salt and pepper, to taste

1 cup chopped carrot

1 cup chopped celery

¾ cup chopped tomato

10 cloves

¼ cup cinnamon

1 teaspoon thyme

1 bay leaf

1 teaspoon myrtle

1 teaspoon rosemary

6 ⅔ cups Cannonau di Sardinia wine

10 ½ oz sliced bacon

¼ cup olive oil

1 (28-oz) can peeled tomatoes, strained and roughly chopped

For the Olive Oil Whipped Potatoes:

2 pounds potatoes

Salt and pepper, to taste

1 ⅓ cups extra-virgin olive oil

5 tablespoons chopped parsley

For the Tomato Tartar:

⅔ oz tomatoes

Salt and pepper, to taste

1 tablespoon extra-virgin olive oil

For the Green Beans:

7 oz green beans

Salt and pepper, to taste

1 tablespoon extra-virgin olive oil

The dish comes from traditional regional Italian recipes. The goat's meat is slowly braised in red wine and Mediterranean spices in a cast iron pan, to make it soft and easy to digest. Other ingredients—potatoes, green beans, and tomatoes—give the goat a contrast of temperatures and sapidity, to make it modern!

- Prepare the goat: Debone the goat, and cut the meat into large pieces. Place it in a nonreactive casserole dish and add salt, pepper, carrots, celery, chopped tomatoes, cloves, cinnamon, thyme, bay leaves, myrtle, and rosemary. Add the wine and marinate for 24 hours.

- Remove meat from the marinade. Strain the marinade into a bowl, reserving the solids and the wine separately.

- Wrap each piece of meat with a slice of bacon, and fry on high heat, browning the bacon. Remove the meat and set aside.

- In a separate pan, heat the olive oil on medium-high and cook the reserved vegetables and herbs until caramelized. Add the pieces of meat and the canned tomatoes. Add the red wine, then slowly braise until the meat is tender, about 2 hours.

- Remove the tender meat from the sauce and cut it into smaller, portion-size pieces. Strain the sauce through a sieve and reserve.

- Make the potato purée: Boil the potatoes in salted water until tender. Peel them and smash with olive oil, salt, pepper, and parsley.

- Make the tomato tartar: Make a cross cut on top of each tomato. Blanch them in boiling water for 8 seconds, then cool in ice water to stop further cooking. Peel the tomatoes, remove and discard the seeds, and cut into small cubes. Marinate with salt, pepper, and extra-virgin olive oil for a few minutes.

- Prepare the beans: Blanch the green beans in boiling water until crisp-tender, then plunge into ice water. Cut the beans into small strips and marinate with salt, pepper, and extra-virgin olive oil.

- To serve, reheat the meat in the sauce. Scoop the mashed potatoes onto the middle of each plate, arrange a few pieces of meat on top, and cover generously with the sauce. Sprinkle the tomato tartar and green beans around the plate.

WINE PAIRING
Cannonau di Sardinia (Italy).

VEDEMA
Santorini, Greece

GRILLED LAMB
WITH GREEN BEANS, TOMATOES, AND SAGE

Serves 4

2 ¼ pounds rack of lamb, trimmed of fat and cut into chops

¾ cup extra-virgin olive oil

1 medium onion, chopped fine

1 clove garlic, chopped fine

1 dried sage leaf

28 ¼ oz ripe tomatoes, roughly chopped, seeds removed

Salt and pepper, to taste

8 ¾ oz green beans

Greece is a nation of small farmers who produce an incredible array of mainly organically farmed cheeses, oils, legumes, and vegetables, supplemented by an array of greens and herbs that grow in the wild. These are the foods that form the base of the traditional Greek regimen, to which they add both variety and nutrition. Lamb and goat (kid) are the traditional meats of holidays and special celebrations.

- Pat the chops dry with paper towels. Place a large skillet over medium-high heat and sear the chops just until caramelized.

- Heat the olive oil in a saucepan over high heat. Add the onions and garlic; sauté them until soft. Add the sage and tomatoes, and bring to a boil; reduce to a simmer and cook until slightly thickened. Season with salt and pepper.

- In a second saucepan, boil the green beans in salted water until crisp-tender. Add the beans to the tomato sauce and simmer gently for 2 to 3 minutes.

- To serve, divide the tomatoes and green beans among 4 shallow bowls, then top with the lamb chops. Finish with freshly ground pepper.

WINE PAIRING
Red Mavrotragano (Santorini).

SANTA MARINA
Mykonos, Greece

FILLET OF SEA BASS
WITH ROASTED PEPPERS, SMOKED AUBERGINE SALAD, AND SAUCE VIERGE

Serves 4

For the Smoked Aubergine Salad:

2 small eggplants

1 tablespoon olive oil

1 clove garlic

Salt and pepper, to taste

2 red bell peppers

2 yellow bell peppers

For the Sea Bass:

½ tablespoon olive oil

4 (5 ½-oz) skinless fillets of sea bass

Fresh basil, for garnish

For the Sauce Vierge:

5 cilantro leaves, chopped

5 tarragon leaves, chopped

1 small tomato, diced

3 tablespoons extra-virgin olive oil

½ tablespoon coriander seeds

¼ cup freshly squeezed lemon juice, to taste

Salt and pepper, to taste

Chef Stathis Thermos, the creative drive and contributor of the new menu at the Santa Marina's redesigned signature Bayview restaurant, proposes this simple yet flavorful Mediterranean dish that expertly combines the lightness of the fish with the flavor of the smoked aubergine with the freshness of the Sauce Vierge to create an ideal light lunch option.

- Make the eggplant salad: Start a grill. Cut each eggplant in half lengthwise and grill until tender, flipping halfway through. Scoop out the flesh and purée it with a little bit of garlic.

- To roast the peppers, hold them with tongs over an open flame until the skins are blistered and charred. Let cool a bit, then peel off the skins. Cut into small pieces.

- Make the sauce: Combine all the ingredients and season with salt and pepper.

- Prepare the fish: Heat 1 tablespoon olive oil over medium heat. Sauté the fillets until cooked through.

- To serve, arrange the roasted peppers on a plate; put the sea bass on top and drizzle with the Sauce Vierge. Spoon the eggplant purée on the plate and garnish with fresh basil.

WINE PAIRING
Athiri Assyrtiko (Santorini, Greece).

TURNBERRY
Turnberry, Scotland

HALIBUT, PEAS, AND PORK JOWL

Serves 2

For the Pork Jowl:

1 whole pork jowl

4 cups plus 2 tablespoons
veal stock

1 bay leaf

4 sprigs thyme

1 bulb garlic, cloves
peeled and crushed

For the Shallot Confit:

5 whole shallots

1 cup olive oil

For the Halibut:

½ pound North Sea halibut

⅓ oz serrano ham, julienned

¼ oz fresh black truffles, sliced

¼ oz wild garlic, whole

For the Pea Purée:

¾ cup chicken stock

7 oz fresh peas, shelled

2 tablespoons unsalted butter

Salt, to taste

For the Pea Velouté:

5 large shallots

1 ¾ oz wild seasonal mushrooms

1 tablespoon unsalted butter

3 ½ oz sea scallops

1 bay leaf

½ bulb garlic

This dish is served in Turnberry's award-winning James Miller Room.

- Cook the pork jowl: Preheat the oven to 325°F. Put a large sauté pan over high heat. When the pan is very hot, sear the pork jowl until golden brown on both sides. Add the veal stock, bay leaf, thyme, and garlic. Put all ingredients into a roasting pan, cover, and cook for about 90 minutes in the oven.

- Make the shallot confit: Put the unpeeled shallots in a pot over low heat and cover with the oil. Cook until soft. Take them out of the oil and let them cool. Peel the shallots and set aside.

- Prepare the halibut: Remove the skin and bones from the fish. Cut out the center piece of meat for use, making sure there is no brown meat. Make 6 small incisions in the fish and stuff with ham, truffles, and wild garlic.

- Make the pea purée: Bring the chicken stock to rapid boil and add the fresh peas. Cook the peas just until soft but still bright green. Drain the peas and put them in a high-speed blender, adding butter gradually and a little stock to achieve a smooth consistency. Cool very quickly over ice to maintain color. Season to taste.

- Make the pea velouté: Place the shallots and mushrooms in a sauté pan over medium-low heat with a little butter and sweat just until soft (do not let them brown). Add the scallops, bay leaf, garlic, and thyme. Add the white wine and simmer to reduce by half. Add the cream, bring to a boil, and remove from heat. Shell the peas and add the shells to the cream, cover, and allow to cool. Strain the mixture, put the liquid in a high-speed blender, and add the fresh peas. Strain again to get rid of any pea shells, and season with salt and lemon juice.

- Prepare the fresh peas: Bring a pot of water to a boil. Add the wild garlic leaves and blanch just until tender and vibrant green; plunge into ice water to refresh; drain. Add the wild garlic leaves and garlic purée to the butter and blend until smooth; pass through a fine sieve and cover with plastic wrap. Bring the chicken stock to a boil and add the garlic butter. Shell the peas and add them to the butter stock, cooking just until the peas are soft.

- Make the pea foam: Take a little of the pea velouté and add a little chicken stock to loosen. Add the lecithin and use a handheld blender to make a foam.

1 sprig thyme

3 tablespoons plus 1 teaspoon white wine

3 tablespoons plus 1 teaspoon double cream

10 ½ oz fresh peas in shells

Salt, to taste

Juice of ½ lemon

For the Fresh Peas:

¾ oz wild garlic leaves

¾ teaspoon garlic purée

4 tablespoons unsalted butter, softened

¼ cup plus 3 tablespoons chicken stock

1 ¾ oz fresh peas in shells

For the Pea Foam:

¾ cup plus 1 tablespoon pea velouté (above)

¾ cup plus 1 tablespoon chicken stock

.03 oz lecithin

- Cook the halibut: Place a nonstick pan over medium heat. Pan-sear the halibut skin side up; flip the fish over and sear the other side. Add a little butter to the pan and place in the oven; bake until cooked through, about 8 to 12 minutes.

- To serve: Heat the pork jowl in a little reduced veal stock until sticky. Smear some pea purée on each plate; place a serving of halibut next to it. Build the garnish on top of the pea purée, starting with the pork jowl, then the shallot confit, then the fresh peas, then a little pool of velouté; finish with the pea foam.

WINE PAIRING

This dish combines the taste of the sea with more earthy peas and pork. To match that complex blend of flavors, a rich and dry white wine like a Condrieu (France), with its minerality and bursting flavors of flowers and ripe yellow fruits, would make the perfect partner. For red wine lovers, a Pinot Noir from Central Otago (New Zealand), which is light and fresh but with a subtle hint of spices to add more contrast, would be a great alternative.

HOTEL CALA DI VOLPE
Costa Smeralda, Italy

SPAGHETTI WITH SPINY LOBSTER RAGÙ

Serves 4
---

2 ½ pounds live lobster

2 cloves garlic, chopped

1 shallot, chopped

8 tablespoons extra-virgin olive oil,
plus more for drizzling

4 teaspoons cognac

½ cup white wine

3 oz parsley, chopped

3 ½ oz cherry tomatoes, diced

5 oz tomato sauce

3 tablespoons plus
¾ teaspoon shellfish broth

Salt and pepper, to taste

10 oz spaghetti

1 tablespoon chopped dill

Spaghetti, fresh tomato, lobster, and all the typical flavors of Mediterranean cuisine are included in this, Cala di Volpe's signature dish, which is really appreciated by the international clientele and jet set that spend their summers in this iconic hotel.

- Place a large pot of water over high heat. When the water comes to a boil, add the lobster. Boil the lobster for 2 minutes, then plunge into ice water to cool. Cut the shell open, and take out the insides, reserving the flesh and discarding the eggs and soft parts.

- Fry half the chopped garlic and the shallot in 3 tablespoons of the oil, then add the lobster shell in pieces. Add the cognac and carefully flambé. Add half of the wine and simmer until it has cooked off. Add a third of the diced tomatoes and all of the tomato sauce and broth. Simmer gently, 15 minutes. Strain the sauce and set aside, keeping it warm.

- Heat the remaining 5 tablespoons oil, the remaining garlic, and the chopped parsley in a pan. Chop the lobster meat and add it; brown the lobster. Pour in the remaining wine and cook off. Then add the remaining diced tomatoes. Season to taste with salt and pepper and keep warm.

- Cook the spaghetti to just al dente, then add it to the sauce and finish cooking. Serve hot, drizzled with olive oil and sprinkled with dill.

WINE PAIRING
Maìa Vermentino di Gallura DOCG Superiore, 2011 (Sardinia).

HOTEL PITRIZZA
Costa Smeralda, Italy

LANGOUSTINES AND PRAWNS
IN ISLAND HERBS

Serves 4

For the Shellfish:

16 fresh langoustines

16 fresh prawns

1 tablespoon extra-virgin olive oil,
plus more for drizzling

½ oz each chopped fresh herbs,
such as thyme, pennyroyal mint,
rosemary, oregano, savory, and
parsley, plus more
for garnish

22 cherry tomatoes, quartered

2 cloves garlic

½ cup fresh tomato sauce: (below)

For the Fresh Tomato Sauce:

9 oz tomatoes

5 tablespoons extra-virgin olive oil

1 tablespoon chopped onion

4 leaves basil

Salt, to taste

Warm bread, for serving

This dish is a tribute to the Mediterranean cuisine and the genuine local products that are carefully chosen daily by our chef, Maurizio Locatelli. The freshness of the langoustines and prawns is the secret of this recipe, which is enriched by fresh herbs and a nice handmade tomato sauce with a personal touch of the chef.

- Prepare the shellfish: Clean the langoustines and prawns, removing the heads and part of the shell; leave the ends of tails.

- Start the fresh tomato sauce: Blanch the tomatoes in boiling water for 8 seconds, then plunge into an ice-water bath. Peel and chop the tomatoes.

- Put a pan over low heat and add 5 tablespoons olive oil, then add the chopped onion and sauté until browned. Turn the heat up to high and add the tomatoes; cook for 20 minutes. Strain the tomatoes, reserving the liquid, and add basil and salt to taste.

- Heat a saucepan over high heat and add 1 tablespoon olive oil. Add the prawns and langoustines along with the chopped herbs. Toss for a few minutes, then add the cherry tomatoes. Add a drizzle of fresh tomato sauce. Cook until the sauce thickens slightly.

- To serve, arrange the langoustines and prawns in nests of tomatoes and dress with more sauce. Finish with a drizzle of extra-virgin olive oil. Serve with thick slices of warm bread and additional herbs.

WINE PAIRING
Nuragus di Cagliari DOC (Italy).

HOTEL ROMAZZINO
Costa Smeralda, Italy

PENNETTE
IN A MARINATED TOMATO SAUCE

Serves 4
---

3 cloves garlic

18 oz cherry tomatoes, quartered

½ cup extra-virgin olive oil, plus
more for drizzling

Salt, to taste

1 ½ oz chopped basil,
plus more for garnish

14 oz plain or ribbed penne pasta

½ onion, finely chopped

1 medium chili pepper, chopped

¼ oz chicken bouillon cube

Pinch of baking soda

This is the favorite dish at the Hotel Romazzino, memorable for its freshness and simplicity. Our creative chef Giovanni Raccagni applies his craft to skillfully transform the best-quality products of Sardinia into an authentic gourmet experience.

- Chop 2 cloves garlic. Place the tomatoes in bowl with ¼ cup olive oil, salt, basil, and the chopped garlic.

- Cook the pasta according to package directions until al dente.

- Meanwhile, put a pan over low heat and add 3 tablespoons oil and 1 clove of garlic. Fry gently, and then add the chopped onion and chopped chili pepper and sauté until browned. Turn the heat up to high and add the basil and tomatoes. Cook for a few minutes. Add salt, the bouillon cube, and a pinch of baking soda. Season as required.

- Drain the pasta and stir into the sauce. Cook the pasta 2 minutes to allow it to absorb the sauce. Toss around and pour into a serving dish; garnish with basil leaves and a drizzle of olive oil.

WINE PAIRING
Semidano di Mogoro DOCG (Italy).

HOTEL MARQUÉS DE RISCAL
Elciego, Spain

CAMEROS CHEESE "TOAST"
WITH APPLES AND HONEY ICE CREAM

Serves 4

For the Cameros Cream Cheese:

4 ½ oz Cameros goat cheese

5 teaspoons milk

1 cup cream

¼ cup sugar

2 sheets gelatin, softened
according to package directions

For the Honey Ice Cream:

2 ¼ cups milk

4 egg yolks

1 egg

¼ cup sugar

¾ cup honey

For the "Toast":

3 sheets phyllo pastry

7 tablespoons unsalted butter, melted

½ cup confectioners' sugar

For the Apples:

2 apples

8 ½ cups water

½ cup sugar

For the Toffee:

²/₃ cup sugar

2 tablespoons butter

5 teaspoons milk

¼ cup cream

Cameros is a hilly area of La Rioja, in Spain. The residents of this area produce traditional goat cheese. The local cheese is consumed fresh with honey that was produced by nearby beehives. This dish is a reminder of this tradition.

- Make the Cameros cream cheese: Heat the cheese, milk, cream, and sugar over low heat, stirring until blended. Stir in the gelatin and chill, 12 hours.

- Make the Honey Ice Cream: Heat the milk over medium heat just until small bubbles form; remove from heat. Whisk the egg yolks, egg, and sugar together. Very slowly pour the egg mixture into the hot milk, whisking. Return to the heat and stir until the custard reaches 182°F; whisk in the honey and remove from heat. Chill in the refrigerator, then freeze the mixture in an ice cream maker according to the manufacturer's directions. Place the ice cream in the freezer until ready to use.

- Make the "toast": Preheat the oven to 350°F. Brush 1 sheet of phyllo pastry with melted butter and sprinkle with sugar. Cover with another sheet of phyllo and repeat, 2 more times. Cut the pastry into circles and place into round 8-cm molds. Bake 10 minutes.

- Prepare the apples: Peel and slice them, then place them in a pot with the water and sugar. Cook them until soft, about 12 minutes. Remove with a slotted spoon.

- Make the toffee: Place the sugar in a dry pan over medium heat; cook just until the sugar liquifies and turns golden brown. Stir in the butter, milk, and cream and cook for 2 minutes.

- To serve, spread the cream cheese on the "toast." Top with apple slices. Paint the apples with toffee. Finish with honey ice cream.

WINE PAIRING

Castillo de Maetierra Melante, 2008. It is a velvety, silky, thick wine, but fresh at the same time—perfect for desserts with honey.

JOSÉ ANDRÉS

Chef and Founder of ThinkFoodGroup

WHAT IS YOUR FAVORITE DISH TO PREPARE?
My favorite dish is always my latest dish. I don't like to repeat things.

WHAT IS YOUR FONDEST MEMORY OF/WITH FOOD?
My first dinner in a starred restaurant. I will always remember these langoustine lasagnes!

WHAT DISH REMINDS YOU OF HOME?
I remember watching my father make paella on Sundays for our family and friends. As a young boy I wanted to be a part of that; I wanted to do it myself. I remember that my brothers and I would be sent out to gather branches for the fire. My dad would always put me in charge of the fire, but never did he let me touch the paella. I would get so angry, and once I finally said, "Why won't you let me cook?" And he told me, "But don't you see, you have the most important job: You are controlling the fire, the heat." That is when I learned what making perfect paella was about, what cooking was about, really. That you have to control the fire!

WHAT IS YOUR FAVORITE FOOD-WINE PAIRING?
I don't like to limit myself. It all depends on my mood. But for pairing, I pay attention to the flavors and the textures and I see what works. But it doesn't always have to be so serious. Sometimes I'll pick something I like, such as a crisp, tangy white wine like an Albariño or a New Zealand Sauvignon Blanc. I tend to like whites with food. Reds are sometimes better by themselves. A red wine can be like a good steak: It doesn't need anything else.

66 Food is about enjoying and sharing moments and memories. 99

HOTEL BRISTOL
Vienna, Austria

BLUEBERRY PANCAKE À LA "KAISERSCHMARRN"

Serves 4

---

5 tablespoons unsalted
butter, softened

2 ½ cups plus 2 tablespoons
all-purpose flour

Pinch of salt

Grated zest of 1 lemon

2 cups plus 2 tablespoons milk

½ cup cream

⅓ cup sugar

1 vanilla bean

8 eggs, separated

7 oz blueberries

Confectioners' sugar, for garnish

There are many stories as to where the name "Kaiserschmarrn" comes from. The most popular is that the chef of Emperor (Kaiser) Franz Joseph I of Austria created this dessert. The Empress Elisabeth did not approve of this Schmarrn, but her husband, the Emperor, grew very fond of it. The original recipe contains raisins, as opposed to the blueberries in the Hotel Bristol recipe. Traditionally the Kaiserschmarrn is caramelized in sugar and then flambéed in rum.

- Preheat the oven to 350°F. Grease a nonstick 8-inch pan with butter.

- Combine the flour and salt in a bowl, then stir in the lemon zest, milk, cream, sugar, and vanilla. Beat the egg yolks and stir them into the batter. In another bowl, use an electric handheld mixer to beat the egg whites until stiff. Fold them carefully into the batter.

- Pour the batter into the prepared pan and sprinkle it with the blueberries. Bake it until golden, about 20 minutes. Then cut the Schmarrn (pancake) into small pieces and sprinkle with confectioners' sugar.

WINE PAIRING
Feiler-Artinger Ruster Ausbruch Pinot Cuvée, 2007 (Austria).

METROPOL PALACE
Belgrade, Serbia

WHITE CHOCOLATE TART
WITH SEASONAL FRUIT

Serves 8

For the Pastry:

4 tablespoons unsalted butter

½ cup confectioners' sugar

2 egg yolks, lightly beaten

1 cup all-purpose flour

For the White Chocolate Filling:

¾ cup whipping cream

1 vanilla bean

1 egg yolk

2 eggs

5 oz white chocolate, chopped

1½ tablespoons unsalted butter

3½ oz of each seasonal fruit variety such as strawberries and plums, sliced, and blueberries

The unique climate of the region and centuries-old tradition of growing the finest, most succulent fruits and berries are presented in this seductive white chocolate tart. It is a true tribute to the farmers who collect the berries and grow the famous Serbian plum, a simple yet rich fruit that is part of a local heritage and considered a symbol of the local people. Metropol Palace created this wonderful dessert to evoke the simplicity of days gone by as well as to give a nod to the best modern European culinary traditions. The richness of the white chocolate and the refined delicacy of blueberries and plum slices make for a veritable journey for the senses.

- Make the pastry: Combine all the ingredients and mix until smooth. Wrap the dough in plastic and leave in the refrigerator to rest, 2 hours.

- Preheat the oven to 325°F. Roll out the dough to an 8-inch circle and fit it into a tart form. Put the form in the freezer for 10 minutes to chill and then bake, 8 minutes. Allow to cool.

- Make the filling: Bring the whipping cream and vanilla bean to a boil; remove from heat, taking out the vanilla bean. Whisk the yolk and eggs in a bowl, then pour the boiled cream into the bowl in a thin stream, stirring constantly. Add the white chocolate and stir until it is melted. Then add the butter, mix well, and pour into the tart crust, spreading it evenly. Bake for 20 minutes. Allow to cool. Pile the fruit on top of the tart and serve.

WINE PAIRING
Kis aromatized Bermet (Serbia) or sweet Samos wine (Greece).

HOTEL GOLDENER HIRSCH
Salzburg, Austria

SALZBURGER NOCKERL
FLUFFY EGG SOUFFLÉ

Serves 4

¼ cup milk

3 tablespoons unsalted butter

½ cup plus 3 tablespoons sugar

8 large egg whites

Pinch of salt

6 egg yolks

⅓ cup all-purpose flour

1 teaspoon vanilla sugar

Grated zest of ½ a small lemon

Confectioners' sugar, for garnish

Austrian cuisine is known for the most delicious treats. Indulgence, culinary art, and a commitment to tradition have always played a key and integral role at the Hotel Goldener Hirsch, which is located in the heart of Salzburg's Old Town. Anyone visiting Salzburg must taste what probably is the city's sweetest temptation: Salzburger Nockerl, a heavenly blend of egg white and sugar, rising with pride before softly melting away on the food lover's tongue.

- Preheat the oven to 475°F. Put the milk, butter, and 1 tablespoon sugar in a flameproof baking pan. Heat over medium heat until slightly caramelized on the edge of the pan. Remove from heat.

- Beat the egg whites with a whisk. Add a pinch of salt and 2 tablespoons sugar and beat the mixture until stiff peaks form. Mix the egg yolks, flour, vanilla sugar, and lemon zest together and then carefully fold into the stiff egg whites.

- Take the creamy mass and use a thin, flexible dough scraper to make 4 pyramid-shaped mounds; place them next to one another in the ovenproof pan. Bake for 10 to 12 minutes, until light golden brown. Dust with confectioners' sugar and serve immediately so the nockerls do not collapse.

WINE PAIRING
A glass of Champagne or a dessert wine.

HOTEL ELEPHANT
Weimar, Germany

ELEPHANT'S KISS

Serves 4

For the Custard:

1 ¼ cups sugar

8 egg yolks

¾ cup plus 2 tablespoons cornstarch

4 ¼ cups milk

1 vanilla bean

For the Cheesecakes:

1 ½ cups custard (above)

1 ¾ cups sour cream

½ oz powdered cream

¼ cup plus 2 tablespoons sugar

2 eggs

1 ½ tablespoons unsalted butter, melted

For the Base:

1 ⅔ oz dark chocolate

1 ⅔ oz hazelnut pulp

1 ⅔ oz Valrhona praline mix

1 ⅔ oz Valrhona éclat d'or (dried crêpes)

4 store-bought chocolate wafer cookies

2 to 3 tablespoons red currant jam

For the Glaze:

12 ⅓ oz white chocolate

⅓ cup rapeseed oil

Enjoy a unique Weimar dessert with Thuringian and Italian accents, created exclusively for our guests as a signature recipe by the Michelin star–awarded chef Marcello Fabbri in the prize-winning kitchen of the restaurant Anna Amalia: sour-cream cake with red-currant filling, roasted Piedmontese hazelnuts, and a white chocolate coating.

- Make the custard: Combine the sugar and the egg yolks; stir in the cornstarch. Heat the milk with the vanilla bean over medium-low heat just until bubbles start to form. Slowly stir half of the milk into the egg mixture, then stir in the second half. Cook the milk mixture again gently until thickened. Remove the vanilla bean and let the custard cool with plastic wrap on the surface so a skin doesn't form.

- Make the cheesecakes: Preheat the oven to 250ºF. Mix the custard filling with the sour cream and cream powder. Beat the eggs with the sugar until frothy and stir carefully into the custard mixture; stir in the melted butter.

- Pour the mixture into 4 muffin molds and bake for about 40 minutes.

- Make the base: Gently melt the dark chocolate in the top of a double boiler or a microwave. Combine it with the hazelnut pulp, the praline mixture, and the éclat d'or and spread it on the chocolate cookies; let it cool. Cut the cookies to the same size as the cheesecake.

- Carefully invert the cheesecakes onto a plate. Coat each bottom with the currant jam, and then attach it firmly to the chocolate base; flip back to right side up. Place in the freezer, at least 2 hours.

- Make the glaze: Melt the white chocolate with the rapeseed oil over low heat, stirring to combine. Place the frozen cakes on a rack, and spread the glaze all over the tops and sides. Let the cakes come to room temperature before serving.

WINE PAIRING
Perrier-Jouët Grand Brut (Champagne, France).

HOTEL GRANDE BRETAGNE
Athens, Greece

SAVARINS IN STRAWBERRY JUICE
WITH MADAGASCAR VANILLA CREAM

Serves 4

For the White Chocolate Cream:

7 oz white chocolate

6 tablespoons plus
2 teaspoons milk

¾ cup heavy cream

1 teaspoon liquid glucose

1 Madagascar vanilla bean

4 sheets gelatin,
softened according to
package directions

For the Strawberry Juice:

17 oz strawberries

¼ cup sugar

For the Savarins:

3 tablespoons unsalted butter,
softened, plus more for molds

¼ cup heavy cream

½ cup milk

2 ½ teaspoons sugar

3 ½ teaspoons active dry yeast

1 cup flour T55

¼ teaspoon salt

1 extra-large egg

Fresh strawberries, for garnish

Mint leaves, for garnish

A light and refreshing recipe for the hot summer days, expertly combining smooth white chocolate cream, savarins, and strawberries.

- Make the white-chocolate cream: Melt the white chocolate gently in a double boiler. Bring the milk, cream, glucose, and vanilla bean to a boil in another pot; remove from heat and add the gelatin. Stir this mixture into the melted white chocolate. Set aside for 12 hours. When ready to use, beat until softened.

- Make the strawberry juice: Arrange the strawberries at the top of a double boiler and sprinkle with the sugar. Cook over medium heat for 2 hours. Strain the strawberries, reserving the juice.

- Make the savarins: Preheat the oven to 350°F. Butter 4 individual savarin baking molds. In the bowl of an electric mixer place the cream, milk, sugar, yeast, flour, and salt. Beat until combined. Beat in the egg and then 3 tablespoons butter. Divide the dough among the molds, smoothing it with your fingers. Let the dough rise for 15 minutes. Bake for 18 minutes. Let cool completely, then unmold.

- To serve: Use a pastry bag to put the white chocolate cream on the savarins. Pour the strawberry juice on each plate and carefully arrange the savarins within. Decorate with random cream dots and pieces of strawberry and mint leaves.

WINE PAIRING
Sweet red Mavrodaphne (Patras, Greece).

SCHLOSS FUSCHL
Salzburg, Austria

CARAMEL-ALMOND SLICE

Serves 2

For the Cremeaux:

6 tablespoons plus 2 teaspoons milk

7 ½ tablespoons cream

3 egg yolks

⅓ cup sugar

2 ⅔ oz milk chocolate, chopped

2 ⅔ oz dark chocolate, chopped

For the Banana Ice Cream:

7 oz peeled baby bananas, chopped

½ cup yogurt

3 tablespoons freshly squeezed
lime juice

Seeds from 1 Tahitian vanilla bean

2 teaspoons rum

¼ cup sugar

For the Candied Almonds:

½ cup cream

1 ¼ cups sugar

½ cup glucose syrup

2 tablespoons unsalted butter

4 ½ oz sliced almonds

For the Pepper Hippe:

7 oz isomalt sugar

4 teaspoons water

1 teaspoon freshly ground pepper

Austrian pastries and desserts enjoy an excellent reputation worldwide. Our sweet delicacies are still prepared by hand with only the most exquisite ingredients.

- Make the cremeaux: Slowly heat the milk, cream, egg yolks, and sugar to 147°F. Pour the milk mixture over the chocolate and stir until chocolate is melted. Mix it in a blender. Refrigerate it for 1 day. Mix it again, then spoon it into a pastry bag.

- Make the ice cream: Mix all the ingredients together with an electric mixer until smooth. Pour it through a strainer, then pour it into cylinder molds and freeze them.

- Make the candied almonds: Bring the cream, sugar, and glucose to a boil; remove from heat. Add the butter and heat the mixture to 230°F. Add the almonds. Pour the caramel on a non-stick baking mat in a rimmed baking sheet. When the caramel becomes firm, cut it into rectangles.

For the Pineapple Chutney:

1 baby pineapple,
peeled and finely diced

Sugar, to taste

1 piece of lemongrass,
finely chopped

⅓ oz grated ginger

1 cinnamon stick

2 teaspoons freshly squeezed
lime juice

1 red chili, seeded and chopped

1 teaspoon pectin

For the Caramel Sauce:

2 cups plus 2 tablespoons cream

⅔ cup glucose syrup

1 Tahitian vanilla bean

1⅓ cups sugar

1 baby pineapple, for serving

2 drops vanilla-infused olive oil,
for serving

4 squares chocolate,
for serving

- Make the pepper hippe: Preheat the oven to 350°F. Combine all the ingredients in a pot and heat to 320°F. Pour it on a non-stick baking mat and let it cool down. Break it into small pieces and blend in a blender until it's in crumbs. Spread the crumbs in an even layer on the non-stick baking mat and bake until light golden brown, about 5 to 7 minutes.

- Make the pineapple chutney: Cook all the ingredients in a pot over medium heat for about 3 to 4 minutes; remove from heat and let it cool down; remove the cinnamon stick.

- Make the caramel sauce: Bring the cream, glucose, and vanilla bean to a boil; strain out the vanilla bean. Place the sugar in a pan over medium heat. Cook just until the sugar becomes golden brown. Add the cream mixture (it will spatter) and heat it, stirring, until it reaches 220°F.

- To serve: Cut a thin slice of pineapple for each serving; shape each into a rectangle and spread with vanilla oil. Top with some pineapple chutney, then candied almonds and pepper hippe, then the chocolate. Place the cremeaux in a piping bag and pipe onto the hippe. Top with a cylinder of banana ice cream, then arrange 2 drops of caramel sauce on each plate.

WINE PAIRING

Emmerich Knoll Riesling Auslese, 2006 (Wachau, Austria).

HOTEL BRISTOL
Odessa, Ukraine

THE PRIMORSKI FIZZ

Serves 1
---

1 ½ tablespoons agave nectar

1 ½ tablespoons water

2 oz Nemiroff Honey
Pepper vodka

1 tablespoon apricot jam

¾ oz lemon juice

1 oz local dry sparkling wine

Ice

Dried apricot skewer, for garnish

Finely grated orange zest,
for garnish

Off the dazzling shores of a mythical port, a city lies seemingly untouched by the ravages of time, young in spirit, yet centuries old. Odessa, the Babylon of the Black Sea, Catherine the Great's southern window on Europe, a cacophony of culture singing a song for the ages on the fine, broad, tree-laden streets of days gone by. Enjoy this unlikely romance with a city, sipping the Primorski Fizz, a remarkable blend of honey-pepper vodka, apricot preserves, lemon juice, and local sparkling wine.

- Combine the agave and water, stirring until the agave is dissolved.

- Pour the agave mixture, vodka, jam, and lemon juice into a cocktail shaker; add ice. Shake hard for 8 to 10 seconds. Add the sparkling wine. Double-strain the cocktail and serve on the rocks in Tom Collins glasses, garnished with skewered dried apricots and a sprinkle of orange zest.

HOTEL KÄMP
Helsinki, Finland

TELLERVO COCKTAIL

Serves 1

For the Lingonberry Agave:

1 cup lingonberry preserves

1 ¾ cups water

2 cups agave

5 cinnamon sticks, broken

20 whole cloves

1 teaspoon ground nutmeg

For the Tellervo Cocktail:

4 ½ teaspoons freshly
squeezed lemon juice

1 small teaspoon
lingonberry preserves

½ egg white

1 oz Lingonberry Agave (above)

2 dashes orange bitters

Splash of absinthe

2 oz vodka

Ice

From deep within the forests of Finland comes the Tellervo Cocktail, a true homage to the rich tapestry of Finnish folklore and the deity of the same name. With a congenial blend of vodka, spiced lingonberry-infused agave, lingonberry preserves, orange bitters, and absinthe, this unique creation soothes the mind and warms the soul.

- Make the lingonberry agave: Combine all the ingredients in saucepan. Bring to a boil, remove from heat, and cover. Let stand for 30 minutes, then strain.

- Make the cocktail: Combine the lemon juice, lingonberry preserves, egg white, lingonberry agave, orange bitters, absinthe, and vodka in a cocktail shaker. Dry-shake (without ice), then add the ice and shake again. Double-strain, and serve straight up in a tulip glass.

HOTEL EXCELSIOR
Naples, Italy

BUONA VITA COCKTAIL

Serves 2

---

2 oz citrus gin

2 oz fresh grapefruit juice

1 oz elderflower cordial

½ oz Campari

Ice

Orange zest, for garnish

A refreshing take on an age-old Italian classic cocktail, the Buona Vita embodies the true essence of the ease and elegance of the Italian lifestyle. It combines the mellow notes of citrus gin, the subtle sweetness of elderflower, and the invigorating brightness of Campari and grapefruit. Here's to life without worry.

- Combine the gin, grapefruit juice, elderflower cordial, and Campari in an 18-oz shaker; add ice. Shake hard for 10 seconds; strain. Serve on the rocks in Tom Collins glasses. Garnish with orange zest.

LATIN AMERICA

PALACIO DEL INKA
Cusco, Peru

FLORENTINE OF QUINOA,
ANDEAN MUSHROOM MIX,
TREE TOMATO COULIS

Serves 10

For the Tree Tomato Coulis:

2 oz tree tomato

1 cup water

2 tablespoons olive oil

Salt and pepper, to taste

For the Quinoa:

4 cups water

2 cups white quinoa

4 tablespoons butter

5 oz red bell pepper, chopped

9 oz Andean mushroom mix,
or any mushrooms, sliced

1 cup cream

7 oz grated Parmesan cheese,
plus more for Parmesan tulip

7 oz baby spinach

Handful of arugula

Salt and pepper, to taste

The dining experience at the Palacio del Inka includes exquisite dishes with fabulous flavors and textures. The chef draws inspiration from ancient Andean cultures, but also uses modern cooking techniques and much creativity to develop delicious and nutritious dishes.

- Make the coulis: Blanch the tree tomatoes briefly, then peel them and remove the seeds. Chop the tree tomatoes and place them in a saucepan with the water. Cook until fruit is soft, mashing with a fork. Purée in a blender. Add the olive oil and salt and pepper, to taste.

- Make the quinoa: Bring the water and the quinoa to a boil; reduce to a simmer, 12 to 15 minutes. Strain and keep warm.

- Melt the butter in a pan and sauté the peppers and mushrooms until soft. Stir in the quinoa, cream, Parmesan cheese, and spinach, cooking until it has the consistency of risotto.

- To serve, pack the quinoa into a ring mold, invert it onto a plate, and take the ring away. Decorate with a Parmesan tulip (spread a little grated Parmesan cheese on a hot grill, cook just until melted, remove and immediately twist into a tulip form) and arugula. Drizzle the tree tomato coulis on the plate around the quinoa.

WINE PAIRING
Baron Philippe de Rothschild Escudo Rojo or Chardonnay
(Valle de Maipo, Chile).

TAMBO DEL INKA
Valle Sagrado, Peru

BAKED GUINEA PIG
WITH KIWICHA TABBOULEH AND BEETROOT PURÉE

Serves 3
---

8 oz beets

Salt and pepper, to taste

3 guinea pig tenderloins,
or rabbit tenderloins

4 teaspoons olive oil

5 ⅓ oz kiwicha (Peruvian
quinoa-like grain)

4 ¼ cups water

3 asparagus spears, sliced thin

1 Peruvian hot chili,
deveined and chopped

1 tablespoon chopped parsley

4 teaspoons freshly
squeezed lemon juice

At Tambo del Inka Luxury Collection Resort & Spa, we try to use as many products as we can from our organic garden, as well as give prominence to local products from Urubamba, Cusco, and from all of the Andes region. This dish represents these core ideas, from our gastronomy to the world.

- Boil the beets until tender, about 1 hour. Drain, reserving some boiled water. Peel the beets and cut them into pieces. Place in the blender and purée, adding a little beet water as needed for a smooth purée. Season to taste with salt.

- Preheat the oven to 325°F. Coat the guinea pig meat with 2 teaspoons of the olive oil; season with salt and pepper. Place it on a nonstick roasting pan and bake, 45 minutes.

- Place the kiwicha in a pot with the water. Bring to a boil, reduce to a simmer, and cook, 15 minutes. Strain and set aside.

- Drop the asparagus into boiling water and boil just for 1 minute; plunge into ice water to stop the cooking. Drain.

- In a bowl, mix the chopped chili and kiwicha with the parsley, the remaining 2 teaspoons olive oil, the lemon juice, salt, and pepper.

- To serve, place the guinea pig on top of the beet purée. Use a ramekin to shape the kiwicha tabbouleh and place beside the meat. Arrange the asparagus alongside the tabbouleh.

SAN CRISTOBAL TOWER
Santiago, Chile

LAMB AGNOLOTTI

Serves 6

For the Lamb Jus:

3 tablespoons olive oil

1 pound whole lamb shank on the bone

Salt, to taste

½ cup chopped Spanish onion

1 large clove garlic, chopped

2 tablespoons chopped celery

¼ cup chopped carrots

¼ oz whole fresh sage leaves

2 tablespoons all-purpose flour

1 ½ tablespoons tomato paste

2 ⅓ cups red wine

2 cups water

A few whole black peppercorns

For the Fresh Pasta Dough:

1 pound Italian 00 flour, or all-purpose
flour, plus more for dusting

⅓ cup semolina

Pinch of salt

5 eggs

For the Filling:

17 ¾ oz cooked lamb (above),
removed from the bone and
chopped into small pieces

⅓ oz shallots, chopped

¼ oz parsley, chopped

⅓ oz fresh morel mushrooms,
soaked, drained, and chopped

¼ oz fresh oregano, chopped

1 ½ teaspoons Dijon mustard

1 cup ricotta cheese

An exceptional dish, prepared with the best ingredients and specially chosen by our executive chef, the Lamb Agnolotti is a classic in Italian cuisine, giving the diner an authentic, home-cooked experience.

- Cook the lamb: Preheat the oven to 350°F. Heat the olive oil over medium heat in a flameproof roasting pan. Season the lamb shanks with salt, and brown them in the roasting pan until crispy on all sides (turn often to avoid burning). Add the onion, garlic, celery, carrots, and sage and continue cooking for 5 minutes. Dust the meat with flour and place the pan in the oven, 5 to 7 minutes. Remove the pan from the oven and stir the tomato paste into the pan juices; place it back in the oven, 15 more minutes.

- Place the lamb, the vegetables, and the pan juices in a medium-size pot. Deglaze the roasting pan with the red wine and pour all the juices into the pot with the rest of ingredients. Add 2 cups water and the peppercorns, and bring to a boil; reduce the heat to a simmer, 3 to 4 hours.

- Meanwhile, make the dough: In a dough mixer or food processor, combine the flour, semolina, and salt. Add 4 eggs and mix until you have achieved a smooth dough that is not sticky. Wrap the dough with plastic wrap and let it rest in the refrigerator, 3 hours.

- Remove the lamb shanks and strain the jus, reserving both. Place the jus in a small pot and reduce until thick, about half its volume. Season to taste, and set the jus aside to be used in the pasta sauce. Reserve the meat for the filling.

- Make the ravioli filling: In a medium mixing bowl place the chopped lamb, shallots, parsley, morel mushrooms, oregano, and Dijon mustard and mix; add the ricotta, Parmesan cheese, salt, and pepper. Mix until all ingredients are evenly combined, and spoon into a piping bag.

- Set a pasta-rolling machine to the thinnest setting, and roll out the dough, laying out the sheets on a table dusted with flour. Using a 3-inch round pastry cutter, cut circles of pasta dough. Whisk 1 egg with a little water. Brush the circles with the egg wash, and place a tablespoonful of lamb mixture off-center on each, then fold the pasta over the filling and press the edges to seal. Set aside on a tray dusted with flour.

- Put a large pot of water over high heat and bring to a boil; add salt.

½ cup grated Parmesan cheese

1 teaspoon sea salt

1 teaspoon freshly ground
black pepper

For the Sauce:

5 tablespoons unsalted butter

1 to 2 cloves garlic, chopped

2 oz pearl onions, peeled

¾ oz fresh morel mushrooms,
soaked, drained, and sliced

1 oz enoki mushrooms

⅓ oz fresh oregano, chopped

¼ oz fresh thyme, chopped

1 cup plus 2 tablespoons
Lamb Jus (above)

For the Garnishes:

¼ oz fresh chives, chopped

⅓ oz thinly sliced red bell pepper

- Make the sauce: In a large sauté pan, melt the butter and add garlic, pearl onions, morel mushrooms, and enoki mushrooms; sauté for 5 minutes. Add the oregano and thyme and cook for 1 more minute. Add the lamb jus and simmer, 3 minutes.

- Boil the agnolotti in batches, cooking until they float to the top, 5 to 7 minutes. Strain and add to the sauce.

- To serve, place 4 to 5 agnolotti on each plate, spoon sauce over them, and garnish with chopped chives and bell peppers.

WINE PAIRING
Chadwick Cabernet Sauvignon, 2005 (Chile).

VILLARRICA PARK LAKE
Villarrica, Chile

OVEN-ROASTED BRISKET

Serves 4

2 ¼ pounds beef brisket

4 cups red wine

1 tablespoon rosemary

6 tablespoons olive oil

⅔ cup coarsely chopped onions,
plus 2 tablespoons finely chopped

⅔ cup coarsely chopped carrots

⅔ cup coarsely chopped celery

7 oz pumpkin, peeled and
cut into medium dice

1 cup Arborio rice

½ cup white wine

3 cups chicken stock

1 tablespoon all-purpose flour

7 tablespoons unsalted butter

3 ½ oz grated Parmesan cheese

¼ cup finely chopped parsley

This is a winter dish. The slow-roasted brisket and pumpkin make it an ideal choice to enjoy for lunch or dinner on a cold rainy day overlooking Villarrica Lake from our restaurant.

- Trim the brisket fat and score the surface. Place the meat in a nonreactive casserole dish with the wine and rosemary and marinate, at least 4 hours. Drain, reserving the marinade.

- Preheat the oven to 225°F. Pour 2 tablespoons of the oil into a flameproof roasting pan over medium-high heat. Sear the meat until golden brown on all sides. Add enough marinade to come halfway up the sides of the pan. Arrange the coarsely chopped onions, carrots, and celery around the beef. Place the pan in the oven and roast, 3 hours, turning the meat over every hour to prevent from drying.

- Remove the meat from the oven and keep it warm. Strain and reserve the meat juices, setting aside for the rice.

- Raise the oven temperature to 400ºF. Toss the diced pumpkin with 2 tablespoons of the oil and season with salt. Place it on a rimmed baking sheet and roast until golden brown and tender.

- Heat the remaining 2 tablespoons oil in a heavy-bottomed pot. Add the finely chopped onion and sweat just until translucent (do not brown). Add the Arborio rice and sauté until coated. Add the wine and cook until reduced by half. Stir in 1 cup of the stock and cook, stirring constantly, until absorbed. Add another cup of stock and do the same.

- In a heavy-bottomed pot heat the butter and flour, stirring, to make a roux. Whisk in the meat juices to make gravy. Cut the brisket into 8 pieces and place in the gravy; keep warm.

- In a heavy-bottomed pot, heat up the rice with 1 cup stock and the pumpkin, and cook until the rice is tender, stirring constantly. Add the butter and cheese and mix well but carefully—do not purée the rice. Finish with some finely chopped parsley.

- Divide the risotto among 4 shallow dishes and top with brisket and gravy.

WINE PAIRING
Serve with an oak-aged Syrah.

ELETTRA WIEDEMANN

Model

> 66 The most memorable meals for me consist of simple ingredients that work together in a way that makes you think, WOW! *What a miracle this is.* 99

WHAT IS YOUR MOST MEMORABLE MEAL?
The meals that blow me away the most are the ones that are the simplest. I think it's easy to make something taste good when it is smothered in sugar, salt, butter, or bacon. The most memorable meals for me consist of simple ingredients that work together in a way that makes you think, *WOW! What a miracle this is.* A simple piece of salmon with lemon and olive oil, avocado on toast with a touch of mayo, an heirloom tomato with the perfect amount of sea salt, a sweet potato with a touch of spice... Things like this blow my mind and are the kind of dishes that I enjoy the most.

WHAT DISH REMINDS YOU OF HOME?
Anything that has to do with pasta, because that is what I ate *exclusively* as a child for years and years.

WHAT WOULD YOU COOK FOR SOMEONE YOU JUST MET?
Probably baked or steamed fish and fresh farmers market greens with one of my made-from-scratch dressings. For dressings, I always love to experiment and pull everything out of my fridge and pantry and mix them together. Nine times out of ten I'll get a great result. When I fail to pull something good together, I go for a great extra-virgin olive oil, a tiny touch of honey and lemon, and balsamic vinegar syrup. For dessert, I usually just break up a bunch of fabulous different chocolate bars and serve with coffee or tea.

WHAT IS YOUR FOOD OF CHOICE WHEN YOU WANT TO INDULGE?
Pasta with my homemade pesto, completely from scratch. It is SO delicious, thick, and decadent. I literally eat spoonfuls of it and bat my hubby away as he likes to swoop in with a spoon or piece of bread.

WHICH DISH DO YOU THINK EMBODIES THE ESSENCE OF PERU?
Obviously ceviche, which we ate on our one day/night in Lima, and it was fantastic. Ceviche feels like a real treat to me because it's something that I would never try myself at home out of fear of undercooking or overdoing it. Other than that, my experience of the food in Peru was that it is hearty, simple, and delicious.

HOTEL PARACAS
Paracas, Peru

GRILLED SEA BASS
WITH VEGETABLE GRATIN, HONDASHI SHALLOTS, LAVENDER SAUCE, AND SAMBUCA FOAM

Serves 4

For the Vegetable Gratin:
1 cup milk
5 tablespoons butter
¼ cup all-purpose flour
Salt and pepper, to taste
1 zucchini, sliced
2 tomatoes, sliced
6 spears asparagus, sliced
1 carrot, sliced
1 tablespoon olive oil
4 oz grated Parmesan cheese

For the Hondashi Shallots:
12 shallots, peeled
3 cups hondashi broth
1 tablespoon butter

For the Lavender Sauce:
2 tablespoons olive oil
¼ cup chopped onions
5 teaspoons chopped garlic
½ cup white wine
¾ cup plus 1 tablespoon cream
⅙ oz lavender flowers
Salt and pepper, to taste
1 tablespoon butter

For the Sambuca Foam:
¼ cup Sambuca
¼ cup fish broth
.05 oz soy lecithin

For the Sea Bass:
1 ¾ pounds sea bass
Salt and pepper, to taste
Extra-virgin olive oil, for serving

In Paracas, we offer a dining experience that highlights dishes based on fish and seafood. We present contemporary Peruvian food inspired by traditional gastronomy to the world.

- Make the Vegetable Gratin: Preheat the oven to 400°F. First, make a béchamel sauce by heating the milk just until bubbles start to form around the edge. In another pot, melt the butter over medium-low heat. Add the flour and cook, stirring constantly, until just pale yellow. Stir in the milk and simmer, stirring, until the sauce thickens. Season with salt and pepper.

- Season the vegetables with salt and pepper. Sauté over high heat with a little olive oil until tender. Place the vegetables in a square baking dish and cover with béchamel sauce. Sprinkle the Parmesan cheese on top and place in the oven. Bake until the sauce is bubbling and the cheese is golden brown, about 6 minutes.

- Prepare the shallots: Place the whole shallots in a pot with the hondashi; simmer over medium heat for 10 minutes, until tender. Remove from heat, add the butter, and whisk the broth to emulsify.

- Make the Lavender Sauce: Heat the olive oil in a frying pan over medium heat, add the onions and garlic, and fry until transparent. Add the white wine and then the cream; cook for 2 minutes. Strain out the solids, pouring the liquid back into the pan. Add the lavender flowers and cook over medium heat for another 2 minutes. Season with salt and pepper. Remove from heat and whisk in the butter.

- Make the Sambuca Foam: Pour the Sambuca and fish broth into a bowl and add the soy lecithin. Use a hand mixer to mix until a foam occurs.

- Grill the sea bass: Prepare a grill. Season the fish with salt and pepper. Grill for three minutes on each side.

- To serve, unmold the vegetable gratin onto a platter, place the sea bass on top, then pour the lavender sauce around the fish. Place the shallots around the platter and decorate with Sambuca foam and a drizzle of olive oil.

WINE PAIRING
Matetic EQ Sauvignon Blanc, 2009 (Chile).

HACIENDA TEMOZON
Yucatán Peninsula, Mexico

COCHINITA PIBIL
PIBIL KEKÉN

Serves 4
---

2 banana leaves

2 ¼ pounds pork loin

½ pound pork chop

½ pound pork leg

1 cup sour orange juice, or a combination of equal parts lemon juice and orange juice

3 ⅓ tablespoons white vinegar

3 ½ oz red achiote paste or annatto

¼ cup chopped white onion

About 8 cloves garlic, chopped

¼ cup diced fresh or canned tomatoes

1 clove

1 tablespoon freshly ground black pepper

1 tablespoon dried oregano

5 teaspoons salt

Refried black beans, for serving

Warm corn tortillas, for serving

Chopped habanero chilis or other hot chilis, for garnish

Yucatán was the first place in America where the natives ate pork; it is popular in many dishes there, for instance the famous Cochinita Pibil. Pibil is a cooking method that involves placing a pot of food on hot coals in a pit and burying them while the food cooks (the Mayan word pib means "buried"). Hacienda Temozon has rescued the culinary tradition of cooking in a pib, or earth oven. This recipe can also be made in a pressure cooker.

- Start a charcoal grill. Place the banana leaves on the grill. When the leaves begin to burn, remove them.

- Spread the smoked banana leaves in a nonreactive casserole baking dish. Cut all the pork into large pieces and put them on top of the banana leaves.

- Combine the sour orange juice, vinegar, and achiote paste; add the onions, garlic, tomatoes, clove, black pepper, oregano, and salt. Pour this mixture over the pork and let marinate for 24 hours in the refrigerator.

- Preheat the oven to 350°F. Wrap the meat in the banana leaves, making sure that the meat is covered. Bake, with the lid on, for 1 ½ hours. The meat should be falling off the bone and the juices reduced to one-third. Remove the meat to a serving dish.

- Serve with refried black beans, warm corn tortillas, and chopped habanero chilis.

WINE PAIRING
Santo Tomás Merlot, 2008 (Ensanada, Baja California, Mexico).

HACIENDA UAYAMON
Yucatán Peninsula, Mexico

CATCH OF THE DAY TIKIN XIC

Serves 4

For the Tikin Xic Sauce:
3 ½ oz achiote paste
¼ cup chopped white onion
3 cloves
4 large cloves garlic
3 red and green bell peppers
1 teaspoon fresh epazote herb
½ cup sour orange juice
½ cup fresh orange juice
1 teaspoon salt

For the Fish:
4 (8-oz) fillets grouper or sea bass
1 tablespoon finely chopped garlic
½ teaspoon salt
½ teaspoon black pepper
4 tablespoons olive oil, for frying

White rice, for serving
Cured onion, for garnish
Roasted tomato, sliced, for garnish
Red bell pepper, sliced, for garnish
Lime wedges, for garnish

Tikin Xic sauce is used as a condiment in Yucatecan cuisine. Originally, cooking Tikin Xic grouper was done on coals of charcoal wood. The basis of this sauce is the achiote paste or annatto. The achiote seed provides the red coloration that characterizes many regional dishes such as cochinita pibil, chicken, and kabik (a beef stew with red sauce). Like other ingredients, annatto was named in the holy books of Chilam Balam.

- Make the sauce: Blend the achiote paste, onion, cloves, garlic, peppers, fresh epazote herb, orange juices, and salt in a blender until smooth. Reserve.

- Prepare the fish: Dry the fillets with a paper towel. Spread them with garlic, salt, and pepper and let stand 10 minutes.

- Pour the sauce over the fish, coating well, and let stand for 5 minutes.

- Heat 2 heavy-bottomed nonstick pans with 2 tablespoons olive oil in each over low heat. Place 2 fish fillets (grouper or sea bass) in each pan and pour all the marinade in the pans with the fish to cook until browned on one side, about 5 minutes. Flip, cover, and leave them to cook for another 5 minutes.

- Serve the fish over white rice, as well as cured onion, roasted tomato slices, sliced bell peppers, and lime wedges, for garnish.

WINE PAIRING
Santo Tomas Merlot, 2006 (Baja California, Mexico).

HACIENDA SANTA ROSA
Yucatán Peninsula, Mexico

POC CHUC
GRILLED OVER CHARCOAL

Serves 6

4 tomatoes

2 whole red onions,
peeled and halved

8 teaspoons salt

3 tablespoons freshly ground
black pepper

5 cloves garlic, chopped

2 ¼ pounds thin pork steaks

Juice of 4 sour oranges or lemons

1 ¾ oz fresh cilantro,
finely chopped

1 cup water

Refried beans, for serving

Sliced avocado or guacamole,
for serving

Warm corn tortillas, for serving

Poc chuc means "grilled over charcoal" in Mayan. The dish originated with the arrival of the Spaniards in the 16th century to the Yucatán; they introduced wild pigs to the area. The Mayans salted the pork for preservation and cooked it with wood and charcoal.

- Preheat the oven to 250°F and start a charcoal grill. Grill the whole tomatoes and the red onion halves for 20 minutes, turning to roast all sides of each vegetable. The onions should be soft through.

- In a large bowl, combine 6 teaspoons of the salt with the pepper and garlic. Spread this on both sides of each pork steak.

- Grill the meat until cooked, about 20 minutes, flipping halfway through.

- Meanwhile, chop the grilled onions. Combine the onions and the sour orange juice in a bowl. Coat the meat with the onions and sour orange juice and keep warm in the oven.

- To make the sauce, finely chop the roasted tomatoes; combine with the chopped cilantro, 1 cup water, and the remaining 2 teaspoons salt.

- Serve the meat with orange juice and onions accompanied with refried beans, sliced avocado or guacamole, and warm corn tortillas.

WINE PAIRING
Flor de Guadalupe, Blanc de Blancs (Valle de Guadalupe, Mexico).

PARK TOWER
Buenos Aires, Argentina

DULCE DE LECHE TASTING

Serves 10

For the Dulce de Leche:

1 (14-oz) can sweetened condensed milk

For the Rogels:

2 cups plus 2 tablespoons all-purpose flour

8 tablespoons unsalted butter

10 egg yolks

Pinch of salt

Cold water, as needed

7 oz store-bought dulce de leche

Confectioners' sugar (optional)

For the Custard:

1 ¼ cups milk

17 oz store-bought dulce de leche

9 eggs, beaten

Dulce de leche ice cream, for serving

Dulce de leche is one of Argentina's most treasured foods. Many Latin American countries claim its provenance. In Argentina, the story of its origin is that it occurred by accident. Lechada, boiled milk and sugar, was often made for tired soldiers during war. The myth is that a woman in Cañuelas, a town in Buenos Aires province, left her lechada cooking too long and it became a dark brown jelly, thus becoming what is now known as dulce de leche.

- Make the dulce de leche: Take the label off the can of sweetened condensed milk and poke a hole on each side of the can at the top. Set the can in a pot and pour in about 1 inch water. Boil for about 2 hours, adding water as necessary. Cool to room temperature, then chill it in the refrigerator for at least 6 hours. Scoop into 10 individual ramekins.

- Start the Rogels: Combine the flour, butter, yolks, a pinch of salt, and a few drops of water to make a semi-hard dough. Let it rest for 1 hour in the refrigerator.

- Make the custard: Preheat the oven to 300°F. Heat the milk with the store-bought dulce de leche until they reach 140°F; remove from heat. Slowly whisk in the eggs, a little at a time. Strain the custard through a sieve. Pour it into 10 individual 2 ⅓-inch round silicone molds. Place the molds in a bain-marie: Fill a roasting pan with water to halfway up the sides of the molds. Bake for 35 minutes. Remove from the oven and let cool completely. Unmold and cut into 1 ½-inch squares.

- Raise the oven temperature to 425°F. Remove the Rogel dough from the refrigerator. Roll it out very thin, and cut it into 2 ⅓-inch circles. Place on a baking sheet and bake, 10 minutes. Remove from the oven and let them cool down.

- To assemble the mille-feuilles, smear the store-bought dulce de leche on top of each Rogel. Sprinkle with confectioners' sugar, if desired. Arrange on each plate one little custard square, a Rogel, a ramekin with the creamy homemade dulce de leche, and a quenelle of dulce de leche ice cream.

WINE PAIRING
The Argentinean classic wine Muscat of Alexandria.

JAVIER GONZÁLEZ ALÉMAN

Chef, Park Tower Buenos Aires

WHAT IS YOUR FAVORITE DISH TO PREPARE?
Any stew where time, patience, and the best seasonal produce are a must, like locro, carbonada, lentejas…

WHAT IS YOUR MOST MEMORABLE MEAL?
An "asado" meal—that's what we call a full barbecue meal—in Mendoza, on a terrace on the Andes hillside.

WHAT IS YOUR FONDEST MEMORY OF/WITH FOOD?
Making pasta with my grandfather, standing on a chair in order to reach the table.

WHAT WAS YOUR FIRST COOKBOOK?
A cookbook for kids called *Quiero Aprender a Cocinar*.

WHAT IS PARK TOWER'S PHILOSOPHY OF FOOD?
Searching for traditional ingredients, treating them with respect, and giving them a touch of distinction by using the best European cooking techniques.

HOW DO YOU CONNECT TO THE REGION'S FOOD/CULTURE?
I am part of various folklore associations—"peñas"—where members meet once a month to share their own handmade food specialties and enjoy local and traditional music and dance. I also love to get lost in local and neighborhood food markets, searching for the newest products and particular producers.

NO ONE SHOULD VISIT ARGENTINA WITHOUT EATING:
Start sharing a tasting of different empanadas, and then a lamb roasted the old way, like in Patagonia, in a cross over the fire, and a memorable sweet end with panqueques de dulce de leche.

> **"I love to get lost in local and neighborhood food markets, searching for the newest products and particular producers."**

HACIENDA SAN JOSE
Yucatán Peninsula, Mexico

CANDIED GREEN PAPAYA DESSERT

Serves 4

1 pound green papaya

3 tablespoons freshly squeezed lime juice

2 cups sugar

4 cups water

2 tablespoons orange flower water

4 scoops vanilla ice cream

Yucatecan cuisine, in particular the desserts, was influenced by European and Creole cuisine. The most well-known and noteworthy dessert is the dulce de papaya, as it highlights the most popular fruit on the Yucatan Peninsula, the Maradol papaya.

- Peel the papaya and cut it into pieces; place in a bowl. Cover it with water, add the lime juice, mix well, and let it soak, 1 hour.

- Drain the papaya, then put it in a large pot. Cover it with fresh water and bring to a boil. When the papaya pieces are al dente, like pasta, remove from heat and drain; allow to cool.

- Place a saucepan over high heat with the sugar and 4 cups water. When it comes to a boil, add the papaya and boil until the liquid forms a light syrup; add the orange flower water.

- Serve the papaya and syrup with vanilla ice cream.

WINE PAIRING
Late Harvest Portal del Alto Moscatel Tardío, 2005
(Valle Central, Chile).

HACIENDA PUERTA CAMPECHE
Yucatán Peninsula, Mexico

MAYAN FIREFLY

Serves 1

For the Mexican Cinnamon-Infused Agave:

1 ½ cups light agave syrup

1 ¼ cups water

2 ½ cinnamon sticks, broken

For the Mayan Firefly:

1 slice jalapeño pepper

1 ½ tablespoons freshly squeezed lime juice

1 ½ tablespoons Mexican Cinnamon-Infused Agave (above)

3 tablespoons pineapple purée

2 oz tequila

Ice

Pineapple leaf, for garnish

Like mystical flash patterns in the southern sky, the Mayan Firefly calls upon centuries of Mexican mythology to create a veritable take on the traditional margarita with fresh pineapple, indigenous cinnamon-infused agave, lime, and a hint of jalapeño. A true homage to the Mayan gods of yesteryear.

- Make the agave infusion: Combine the agave and water. Toast the broken cinnamon sticks in a dry pan until smoking. Place in a pot and add the agave and water. Bring to a boil; reduce the heat, cover, and simmer for 45 minutes. Strain, reserving the syrup.

- Make the cocktail: Muddle the jalapeño. Combine the jalapeño, lime juice, agave infusion, pineapple purée, and tequila in an 18-oz metal shaker. Add ice and shake hard for 10 seconds. Strain.

- Serve on the rocks in double old-fashioned glass. Garnish with a pineapple leaf.

NORTH AMERICA

THE EQUINOX
Manchester Village, Vermont, USA

LOBSTER ROLL

Serves 6

Salt and pepper, to taste

3 (1 ¼-pound) live lobsters

1 stalk celery, finely chopped

2 tablespoons freshly
squeezed lemon juice

1 tablespoon chopped
fresh chives

2 to 3 tablespoons mayonnaise

6 (4-oz) brioche rolls,
halved horizontally

2 tablespoons unsalted butter,
at room temperature

*The lobster meat can be prepared a day ahead. Just cover it and keep in
the refrigerator. Toss it with the remaining ingredients just before serving.*

▪ Fill a large pot with 1 inch water; bring to a boil and salt generously.
Add the lobsters, cover, and cook until bright red, 8 to 10 minutes.
Transfer the lobsters to a rimmed baking sheet and let cool.

▪ Crack the lobster shells, pick the meat from the tail and claws, and
cut into ½-inch pieces. Combine the lobster with celery, lemon juice,
chives, and 2 tablespoons mayonnaise; season with salt and pepper
and add more mayonnaise, if desired.

▪ Heat a large skillet over medium heat. Spread the cut sides of the buns
with butter. Place butter side down on the hot skillet and cook until
golden, about 2 minutes; fill with lobster mixture.

WINE PAIRING
Sonoma-Cutrer Russian River Ranches Chardonnay (Sonoma,
California), Calera Viognier (Central Coast, California), or
Esser Sauvignon Blanc (Monterey, California).

THE LIBERTY
Boston, Massachusetts, USA

VEAL MEATBALL SLIDERS
WITH CRISPY SAGE

Serves 6

---

1 tablespoon olive oil

1 medium onion, finely chopped

5 cloves garlic, finely chopped

1 pound ground veal

1 tablespoon coarsely chopped sage

2 tablespoons hot chili sauce

¼ cup bread crumbs

2 large eggs, lightly beaten

Kosher salt, to taste

1 cup (2 sticks) butter

2 tablespoons water

¼ cup grated Parmesan cheese

Canola oil, for frying sage leaves

12 sage leaves

12 brioche slider buns, warmed

The Veal Meatball Sliders with Crispy Sage is the most popular dish at Clink. Our guests absolutely love them! With this dish, diners can experience chef Joseph Margate's enthusiasm for umami, the fifth taste most commonly described as the sensation of savoriness on the tongue.

- Preheat the oven to 425°F.

- Heat the olive oil in a large skillet over medium heat. Add the onion and garlic and cook until translucent, about 5 minutes. Remove from heat and let cool.

- Place the onion and garlic mixture in a large bowl and add the ground veal, chopped sage, chili sauce, bread crumbs, eggs, and salt. Knead mixture until well combined. The mixture can be made ahead and stored in the refrigerator at this point.

- Roll the meat mixture into 2-inch balls, transferring them to a rimmed baking sheet. Cook them in the oven for 10 minutes.

- Melt the butter over medium heat and whisk in 2 tablespoons water; do not allow the mixture to boil. Remove from heat. Whisk in the cheese to form an emulsion.

- Heat about 2 inches canola oil in a pan over medium-high heat to 340°F. Fry the sage leaves in the hot oil until crispy, about 45 seconds.

- Toss the meatballs in the butter-Parmesan emulsion and serve each one in a warmed brioche slider roll along with a fried sage leaf.

WINE PAIRING
A classic red Burgundy.

SLS HOTEL AT BEVERLY HILLS
Los Angeles, California, USA

TUNA AVOCADO CEVICHE ROLL

Serves 4

For the Coconut Ceviche Dressing:

¼ cup freshly squeezed lime juice

1 (3-inch) piece ginger, peeled

1 tablespoon Dijon mustard

1 (12-oz) can coconut milk

Salt and pepper, to taste

1 ¾ cups canola oil

For the Tuna Avocado Ceviche Roll:

6 oz sushi-grade tuna, diced small

½ cup Coconut Ceviche Dressing, plus more for plating (above)

¼ cup small-diced red onion

¼ cup small-diced jicama

2 tablespoons minced chives

Maldon sea salt, to taste

Extra-virgin olive oil, as needed

1 avocado

¼ cup corn nuts or corn chips, for garnish

Cilantro leaves, for garnish

Grated zest and juice of 1 lime, for garnish

The market-fish tuna ceviche is the perfect combination of flavors. The ceviche is made daily with fresh market tuna, which varies from day to day depending on the season. It is then marinated in coconut dressing, delicately wrapped in thinly sliced avocado, and garnished with micro cilantro and corn nuts to add depth and texture to the dish.

- Make the dressing: In a blender, add all of the ingredients except for the oil. Pulse until well blended. When fully incorporated, slowly add the oil and purée to emulsify. Strain the dressing into a container, season with salt, and store in the refrigerator.

- Make the ceviche: In a small bowl, mix the diced tuna with ½ cup dressing, the red onions, jicama, chives, and salt to taste.

- Place 4 squares of parchment paper on a baking sheet and lightly oil them. Carefully peel the skin from the avocado and pit it, quartering the flesh lengthwise. Using a vegetable peeler, peel long, thin slices from a piece of the avocado. Place the slices on 1 square of parchment, overlapping by ¼ inch. Repeat with the remaining avocado to make a total of 4 avocado sheets.

- Season the avocado sheets with salt. To assemble the avocado rolls, place 1 ½ oz marinated tuna in a straight line on the long edge of each sheet. Using the paper as you would a sushi roller, roll the avocado sheets around the tuna once, carefully peeling away the paper while rolling.

- Spoon a small amount of the dressing in the center of each of 4 small plates, and place an avocado roll on top. Garnish each plate with 1 tablespoon of the corn nuts or corn chips, cilantro leaves, a few drizzles of oil, sea salt, a dash of lime juice, and pinch of lime zest.

WINE PAIRING
Jäger Smaragd Grüner Veltliner, 2011 (Austria).

RUTH REICHL

Writer and Editor

66 The wonderful thing about New York is that is has been so profoundly influenced by the waves of immigrants who have come flooding through. Walking the neighborhoods you can taste this history. 99

WHAT IS YOUR FAVORITE DISH TO PREPARE?
Pie. Of any kind. But especially apricot pie.

WHERE DID YOU LEARN TO COOK?
My mother was such a terrible cook that I started cooking, seriously, when I was very young. Anything to keep her out of the kitchen. The cover of my memoir, *Tender at the Bone,* has a picture of me cooking at age 7, and you can see that I am very serious about it. The great thing about learning to cook young is that you're fearless; it never occurs to you that you might make a mistake. On top of that, everyone thinks young cooks are so adorable that they tell you it was great, even when it wasn't.

WHAT IS YOUR FONDEST MEMORY OF/WITH FOOD?
The first time I had a soufflé. I was 12, at the home of a friend whose father was a great gourmet, and I felt as if he was feeding me magic. The sense of that soft, rich soufflé evaporating in my mouth—I took one bite, and then another. I couldn't get enough.

WHAT IS A DISH YOU CANNOT LIVE WITHOUT?
Good fresh bread with cold sweet butter. The best food on earth.

WHAT INGREDIENTS DEFINE NEW YORK?
Oysters are probably the city's most iconic dish; they pretty much made Manhattan. In 1880, New Yorkers were eating 700 million oysters a year in the hundreds of oyster parlors that dotted the city. Today no visitor should miss the Grand Central Oyster Bar. But in subsequent years immigrants brought new foods that defined the city. Bagels. Lox. Pastrami. Hot dogs. Pizza. Tacos. Today's definitive foods? Halal curry chicken. And Cronuts.

HOW DOES THE REGION'S CULTURE CONNECT TO ITS FOOD/ FLAVORS? The wonderful thing about New York is that it has been so profoundly influenced by the waves of immigrants who have come flooding through. Walking the neighborhoods you can taste this history. Start downtown and wander through Chinatown, stopping for dim sum at the Nom Wah tea parlor, which has been here since the fifties. Move up through Little Italy, taking a stroll through Di Palo's extraordinary cheese shop. Keep moving north, where you'll find that the old Jewish shops of the Lower East Side are still thriving; stop at Katz's Deli for a pastrami sandwich, then go down the street to Russ and Daughters, which has been selling the city's best smoked salmon (and caviar) for more than a hundred years.

THE CHATWAL
New York, NY, USA

STEAK TARTARE
WITH CAPERS, RYE, AND BONITO FLAKES

Serves 4

For the Steak Tartare:

1 pound Wagyu hanger steak, trimmed and diced fine

2 tablespoons minced shallots

Grated zest of 1 lemon

1 tablespoon chopped chives

2 tablespoons extra-virgin olive oil

2 teaspoons kosher salt

½ teaspoon freshly ground black pepper

For the Sauce:

1 egg yolk

1 tablespoon champagne vinegar

1 clove garlic, minced

1 teaspoon bonito flakes

⅓ cup vegetable oil

For the Potato Chips:

Canola oil, for frying

3 fingerling potatoes

1 egg, hard-boiled, yolk and white separated, for garnish

¼ cup rye bread crumbs, toasted, for garnish

4 large caper berries in brine, sliced, for garnish

Toasted rye bread, for serving (optional)

Steak Tartare is a classic menu item at The Lambs Club Restaurant & Bar and one of chef Geoffrey Zakarian's favorite dishes to make. Wagyu hanger steak is the preferred beef choice, but regular hanger steak can work if Wagyu cannot be sourced. Due to the higher fat content of the beef, which is what ultimately imparts the flavor, it is crucial to dice the meat very small so it can easily be eaten.

- Prepare the Steak Tartare: In a medium-size bowl, combine with a spoon the beef, shallots, lemon zest, chives, olive oil, salt, and pepper. Mix vigorously until the oil is emulsified and the beef appears to be creamy.

- Make the sauce: In another medium-size bowl combine the raw egg yolk, champagne vinegar, minced garlic, and bonito flakes. Slowly drizzle in the vegetable oil, whisking vigorously until emulsified and creamy.

- Make the potato chips: Place a pot of canola oil over medium-high heat. Heat the oil to 350°F. Using a mandoline on the thinnest setting, slice the fingerling potatoes. Fry the potato slices until golden brown, about 5 minutes.

- To serve, spoon the beef into individual molds, then unmold one on each plate; drizzle sauce around the plate, and sprinkle a few potato chips on top. Divide the garnishes evenly among the plates. Serve with toasted rye bread or no bread at all.

WINE PAIRING

A classic Sauvignon Blanc, either from Sancerre, Bordeaux, or even New Zealand, and even other varietals such as Albariño and Godello can elevate the dish.

THE BALLANTYNE
Charlotte, North Carolina, USA

TUNA CRUDO

Serves 4

For the Yuzu Espuma:

2 tablespoons yuzu juice

2 tablespoons sudachi juice

¼ cup pineapple juice

½ teaspoon tapioca maltodextrin

1 teaspoon xanthan gum

1 tablespoon Versawhip

2 tablespoons palm sugar syrup

For the Mandarin Vinaigrette:

1 cup mandarin orange supremes

¼ cup rice vinegar

2 tablespoons pickled ginger

1 shallot, chopped

1 cup olive oil

¼ cup honey

Kosher salt, to taste

White pepper, to taste

For the Tuna Loin:

1 pound sushi-grade #1 tuna loin

¼ cup Mandarin Vinaigrette (above)

8 oz hearts of palm, sliced on
a bias to ¼ inch thick

8 oz cantaloupe, sliced into
1-inch-by-3-inch pieces

2 teaspoons pink peppercorns

Kosher salt, to taste

¼ cup Yuzu Espuma (above)

1 oz micro cilantro

*This bright, citrusy crudo is intended to be a reflection of summer.
The dish effortlessly balances raw and crunchy textures against fruity
and savory flavors. Elegant simplicity.*

- Prepare the Yuzu Espuma: Mix all the ingredients together in a
  blender. Place the espuma mixture into a siphon and charge with
  nitrogen. Chill in the refrigerator.

- Make the Mandarin Vinaigrette: Emulsify the mandarin supremes,
  rice vinegar, pickled ginger, shallot, olive oil, and honey in a blender.
  Season the vinaigrette to taste, pour into a squirt bottle, and chill.

- Prepare the tuna loin: Slice the fish into sashimi-style pieces, cutting
  between the connective tissue. Season lightly with the Mandarin
  Vinaigrette and hold chilled.

- To serve, chill 4 plates. Combine 3 to 4 tuna slices, 4 slices heart of
  palm, and 4 slices cantaloupe per serving, arranging on each plate.
  Season with vinaigrette, crushed pink pepper, and salt. Garnish with
  espuma, crushed pink pepper, vinaigrette, and cilantro.

WINE PAIRING
Viognier.

HOTEL IVY
Minneapolis, Minnesota, USA

TOMATO-BASIL SOUP
WITH MINI GRILLED GOAT CHEESE SANDWICHES

Serves 6

For the Tomato Soup:

1 to 2 tablespoons vegetable oil

1 small onion, medium-diced

1 (28-oz) can peeled
San Marzano tomatoes with juice

½ pound canned roasted
red peppers

2 cloves garlic

1 cup red wine

½ teaspoon dried oregano

¼ cup fresh basil chiffonade,
plus more for garnish

1 tablespoon butter

1 tablespoon sugar

1 cup heavy cream

Salt and pepper, to taste

Sour cream, for garnish

For the Mini Goat
Cheese Sandwiches:

12 slices bread of your choice

2 cups whipped
chèvre goat cheese

Unsalted butter

The creaminess of the soup is a perfect match for these grown-up grilled cheese sandwiches. Tasty enough to chase away the Minnesota winter chills.

- Make the soup: Sweat the onions in the oil until a little liquid forms but the onion is not yet translucent. Add the tomatoes (with juice), roasted red peppers, garlic, wine, oregano, fresh basil, butter, and sugar. Bring to a simmer; cook until the flavors infuse, 30 to 45 minutes. Stir in the cream. Purée the soup and season to taste with salt and pepper. Keep warm.

- Make the sandwiches: Spread a generous amount of goat cheese on one side of each piece of bread. Spread butter on the other side of each piece, and grill butter side down, open-faced, until golden brown and the cheese begins to soften. Join the pieces together to make 6 sandwiches. Cut the sandwiches into quarters widthwise to form sandwich sticks.

- To serve, ladle the soup into bowls and garnish with a dollop of sour cream and a scattering of fresh basil chiffonade on top. Arrange the sandwich sticks around the bowls.

PALACE HOTEL
San Francisco, California, USA

GARDEN COURT CRAB SALAD

Serves 1

For the Dressing:

1 egg yolk

2 tablespoons white wine vinegar

2 tablespoons freshly squeezed lemon juice

1 clove garlic, minced

4 anchovy fillets, minced

1 green onion, chopped

2 tablespoons parsley, chopped

2 tablespoons chives, chopped

¼ cup tarragon, chopped

2 cups salad oil

For the Salad:

2 oz seasonal lettuces

½ oz crème fraîche

5 ½ oz Dungeness crabmeat, picked over for shells

1 cucumber ribbon

¼ avocado

2 ½ cherry tomatoes

A few thin slices red bell pepper

5 Blue Lake beans, blanched

The Palace Crab Salad has been on our menu for decades. While the recipe has evolved over the years, it continues to be the favorite item on the Garden Court menu. It truly represents the Palace and everything we are committed to offering our guests: locally sourced, sustainable products that are indigenous to San Francisco—literally found right in our own backyard. The updated presentation and farm-fresh ingredients bring innovation to the historic recipe while still honoring tradition. That balance is signature to the Palace Hotel culinary experience.

- Make the dressing: Combine all the ingredients except the oil in a food processor. Turn on the processor and slowly add the oil.

- Make the salad: Toss the lettuce with a small amount of the dressing until well coated.

- Mix the crème fraîche with the crabmeat. Wrap the mixture tightly with the cucumber ribbon.

- Pile the lettuce on the plate and garnish with avocado, cherry tomatoes, bell pepper, and Blue Lake beans.

WINE PAIRING

Cakebread Sauvignon Blanc (Napa Valley, California) or Domaine Bernard Moreau et Fils Chassagne-Montrachet (Côte de Beaune, France).

THE NINES
Portland, Oregon, USA

RABE AND ROMANESCO SALAD
WITH ENGLISH MUFFIN CROUTONS

Serves 8

---

8 oz Romanesco broccoli,
broken into florets

8 oz broccoli rabe,
roughly chopped

1 ½ egg yolks

¼ cup roasted garlic purée

2 tablespoons Dijon mustard

½ teaspoon red chili flakes

3 tablespoons red wine vinegar

½ tablespoon kosher salt

1 tablespoon chopped
fresh oregano

1 ¼ cups vegetable oil

1 cup extra-virgin olive oil,
plus more for drizzling

One head petite romaine heart,
chopped into large chunks

2 oz chopped basil

English muffins, diced
and toasted, for croutons

At Urban Farmer, the summer bounty of the Pacific Northwest brings its surprises. This speciality broccoli brings both visual appeal through nature's symmetry and sweet crunch from the summer sun.

- Blanch the Romanesco broccoli and rabe separately in boiling water just until tender. Plunge into ice water to stop the cooking; drain well.

- Whisk together the egg yolks, garlic purée, mustard, chili flakes, vinegar, salt, oregano, vegetable oil, and olive oil.

- Toss the Romanesco broccoli, rabe, lettuce, and basil with enough dressing to coat well. Place the English muffin croutons on top; finish with sea salt and an extra drizzle of extra-virgin olive oil.

WINE PAIRING
WillaKenzie Estate Pinot Noir Pierre Léon (Washington, USA).

THE FAIRFAX AT EMBASSY ROW
Washington, District of Columbia, USA

SPRING PEA RISOTTO

Serves 6

3 shallots, minced

5 tablespoons extra-virgin olive oil

2 cups Arborio rice

½ cup white wine

3 cups vegetable stock, simmering

¼ cup grated Parmesan cheese

4 oz fresh shucked peas

1 teaspoon truffle oil

Salt and pepper, to taste

For this spring risotto, we use available vegetables that are in season at the Dupont Farmers Market—in this instance, fresh-shelled peas. For our go-to vegetarian dish, we omit the Parmesan cheese to make it truly vegan.

- Sauté the shallots over medium-low heat in olive oil until soft. Add the rice, stirring for 3 to 5 minutes to coat the rice with oil; do not let the onions or rice brown.

- Pour in the white wine and about a quarter of the vegetable stock. Slowly stir the rice until all the liquid is absorbed; continue stirring and keep adding the hot stock another quarter at a time. Continue to stir over low heat for an additional 15 minutes, keeping the rice creamy.

- Remove from the heat and add the Parmesan cheese, peas, and truffle oil. Season to taste with salt and pepper.

WINE PAIRING
Steinfeld Grüner Veltliner, 2011. A young, spicy, and refreshing Austrian wine.

THE ROYAL HAWAIIAN
Waikiki, Hawaii, USA

POTATO-SCALED HAWAIIAN ISLAND FISH AND KONA ABALONE

Serves 4

For the Bouillabaisse:

2 cups diced celery

2 ½ cups julienned fennel

4 cups julienned onions

2 tablespoons minced garlic

½ teaspoon saffron

2 tablespoons extra-virgin olive oil

½ cup white wine

1 tablespoon tomato paste

1 ½ quarts clam juice

½ cup kaffir lime leaves

1 Roma tomato, chopped

¼ pound fish scraps, preferably white fish

2 tablespoons brandy

2 tablespoons Pernod

1 tablespoon paprika

1 tablespoon curry powder

½ tablespoon Thai red curry paste

For the Fish:

1 Yukon gold potato

¼ cup clarified butter, melted

2 tablespoons cornstarch

4 (3-oz) onaga fillets

Salt and pepper, to taste

1 egg yolk

2 tablespoons cottonseed oil

For the Garnish:

2 abalone, steamed 6 minutes, diced

1 fennel bulb, diced

1 tomato, peeled and diced

4 sprigs chervil

This recipe blends island flavors with classic techniques. Hawaiian cuisine is a melting pot of ethnic backgrounds that come together to make some of the best flavors in the world. We call it Pacific Island cuisine. Here is a taste.

- Make the bouillabaisse: Sweat the celery, fennel, onions, garlic, and saffron in the olive oil just until soft; do not brown them. Deglaze with white wine. Add the tomato paste, clam juice, kaffir lime leaves, tomato, and fish. In a separate pan, combine the brandy, Pernod, curry powder, paprika, and red curry paste. Boil briefly to cook out the alcohol; add this to the broth. Simmer, 45 minutes. Blend with an immersion blender, then pass through a sieve. Keep warm.

- Prepare the fish: To make the scales, use an apple corer to trim the potato lengthwise into a cylinder. Slice the cylinder paper-thin with a mandoline. Blanch the potato slices and drain; reserve. Mix the melted clarified butter and cornstarch together; reserve.

- Season the fish with salt and pepper. Coat one side with the egg yolk. Coat the fish "scales" in the cornstarch mixture, then arrange them in a scaled pattern on each fillet.

- Fry the fish fillets, scales side down, in hot cottonseed oil until golden brown; turn carefully, and cook until done.

- Place the diced abalone, fennel, and tomatoes in a circle in a shallow bowl; place the fish in the center and garnish with chervil. Serve the bouillabaisse in bowls alongside.

WINE PAIRING
Trefethen Dry Riesling (Napa, California).

THE PHOENICIAN
Scottsdale, Arizona, USA

WESTERN COWBOY BURGER

Serves 4

For the Steak Sauce:
¾ cup ketchup
¼ cup horseradish
⅓ cup chipotle purée
2 tablespoons Dijon mustard
2 cups Worcestershire sauce
½ cup brown sugar
¼ cup honey
¼ cup soy sauce

For the Burgers:
8 strips of bacon
2 pounds ground chuck
(80 percent lean)
Salt and pepper, to taste
1½ tablespoons canola oil
4 slices sharp cheddar cheese
4 challah burger buns
Lettuce
Sliced tomatoes
Sliced onions
1 jalapeño, finely sliced
8 battered and fried onion rings
Steak Sauce (above)

The authentic taste of the American Southwest comes through in this hamburger, sure to please the heartiest of appetites.

- Make the steak sauce: Combine the ingredients in large bowl and whisk until sugar is fully dissolved. Cover and store until ready to use.

- Heat a gas grill to high, or heat coals in a charcoal grill. Cook the bacon until crisp.

- Make the burgers: Divide meat into 4 equal portions. Form each portion loosely into a ¾-inch-thick burger, and make a deep depression in the center with your thumb. Season both sides of each burger with salt and pepper. Brush the burgers with oil. Grill the burgers to desired doneness inside and slightly charred on the outside. Top the burgers with cheese during last minute of cooking.

- Assemble the burgers with lettuce, tomato, and sliced onion on the bottom bun. Top each with a burger and add sliced jalapeño, bacon strips, and fried onion rings. Drizzle with steak sauce and top with buns.

WINE PAIRING
Fruitful California Zinfandel is a must-have with burgers.

THE CANYON SUITES AT THE PHOENICIAN
Scottsdale, Arizona, USA

ARIZONA CHILI RISTRAS

Serves 1

2 oz tequila

1 ½ oz pineapple purée

1 oz chipotle chili
cilantro-infused agave

1 oz freshly squeezed lime juice

Ice

Chili pepper, for garnish

Grated lime zest, for garnish

Across Arizona and the American Southwest, families hang clusters of peppers, called chili ristras, welcoming friends and family to their homes. The Chili Ristras cocktail, an ode to the Arizona chili pepper, represents a sense of place with the warmth of chipotle- and cayenne chili–infused agave, and the friendly, familiar flavors of pineapple and cilantro, all mixed with a beautiful tequila. Welcome home.

Place the tequila, pineapple purée, infused agave, and lime juice in a cocktail shaker; add ice, shake, and strain into a double old-fashioned glass. Serve on the rocks, garnished with a skewered chili pepper and grated lime zest.

THE US GRANT
San Diego, California, USA

S'MORES

Serves 8

Providing a contemporary twist on the classic dessert, The Grant Grill serves a deconstructed version, featuring brûléed marshmallow, graham cracker ice cream, caramelized bananas, and rich chocolate fudge.

For the Graham Cracker:
¼ cup all-purpose flour
2 tablespoons whole wheat flour
Pinch of baking powder
2 tablespoons butter, softened
½ teaspoon honey
½ tablespoon brown sugar
Pinch of salt
Pinch of ground cinnamon
½ tablespoon granulated sugar

For the Vanilla Ice Cream:
½ cup sugar
¼ teaspoon salt
7 egg yolks
1 cup milk
1 cup heavy cream
½ vanilla bean, split and scraped, seeds reserved
Graham Cracker crumbs (above)

For the Marshmallows:
¼ cup water
¼ cup corn syrup
¾ cup sugar
3 sheets gelatin, soaked in ice water until pliable
2 egg whites

For the Fudge Sauce:
½ cup heavy cream
1 ¼ tablespoons corn syrup
3 oz 55% chocolate, chopped

For the Caramelized Bananas:
½ cup heavy cream
¼ cup brown sugar
Salt
2 tablespoons butter
2 ripe bananas, sliced

- Make the graham cracker: Preheat the oven to 325°F. Sift the flours and baking powder together. In a separate bowl, cream the butter, honey, brown sugar, and salt together. Add the flour mixture to the butter mixture and mix until crumbly.

- Roll out the dough to a ¼-inch thickness, then carefully transfer it to a small baking pan lined with parchment paper. Mix the cinnamon and sugar together and sprinkle over the graham cracker. Bake until golden brown, 7 to 10 minutes. Once cool, crumble into crumbs.

- Make the ice cream: Place the sugar, salt, and egg yolks in a bowl and mix well.

- Bring the milk, cream, and vanilla seeds to a simmer. Pour about ½ cup hot milk into the egg mixture, whisking, then slowly whisk the now-warm egg mixture back into the hot milk. Cook over medium-low heat, stirring constantly, until thickened enough to coat the back of a spoon. Chill the mixture.

- Make the ice cream according to your ice cream maker's directions. Fold the graham cracker crumbs into the ice cream (reserving some for the garnish) and chill in the freezer until ready to use.

- Make the marshmallows: Place the water, corn syrup, and sugar in a pot and cook over medium-high heat to 235°F on a candy thermometer.

- Add the gelatin to the egg whites and whip with a handheld mixer on medium speed until the beaters start to leave tracks in the egg whites. Then slowly and very carefully pour the cooked sugar in a small stream into the egg white mixture while mixing on high speed. Whip until the bottom of the mixing bowl is no longer warm to the touch.

- Spread the marshmallow on a baking sheet lined with parchment paper; refrigerate until firm. Once firm, cut out 8 circles.

- Make the fudge sauce: Heat the cream and corn syrup together over low heat until bubbles just start to form around the edges. Pour this over the chopped chocolate, stirring, until the chocolate melts.

- Prepare the bananas: Heat the cream, brown sugar, salt, and butter together over low heat, cooking until the mixture has reached a golden brown color. Add the bananas, cooking them just slightly.

- To serve, brush some fudge sauce onto each plate. Place a marshmallow atop the fudge sauce, and brown the marshmallows, using a torch, until golden brown. Add the caramelized bananas and ice cream, and sprinkle with crumbled graham crackers for garnish.

THE ST. ANTHONY
San Antonio, Texas, USA

THE TRIPLE S

Serves 1

---

1 jalapeño chili

2 oz tequila

1 oz lime juice

1 oz watermelon purée

¾ oz agave

Ice

Hickory-smoked salt, for garnish

The rich tradition of Texas barbecue with sweet, spicy, and smoky flavors is mirrored in this Lone Star State cocktail: the Triple S. Big, juicy watermelon combined with spicy jalapeño chili, hickory-smoked salt, lime, and tequila meld together and transform into a libation with a spirit as big as Texas itself.

- Muddle chili in cocktail shaker, and add remaining ingredients. Add ice, shake, and strain; serve on rocks in a double old-fashioned or rocks glass rimmed with hickory-smoked salt.

METRIC CONVERSIONS CHART

VOLUME

1 tsp. = ⅓ tablespoon = ⅙ fl. oz. = 4 ml

1 Tbsp. = 3 teaspoon = ½ fl. oz. = 15 ml

⅛ cup = 2 tablespoons = 1 fl. oz. = 30 ml

¼ cup = 4 tablespoons = 2 fl. oz. = 50 ml

⅓ cup = ¼ cup plus 4 tsp. = 2¾ fl. oz. = 75 ml

½ cup = 8 tablespoons = 4 fl. oz. = 125 ml

¾ cup = 10 tablespoons = 6 fl. oz = 175 ml

1 cup = ½ pint = 8 fl. oz. = 250 ml

1 pint = 16 fl. oz. = 2 cups = 500 ml

1 quart = 32 fl. oz = 2 pints

1 liter = 34 fl. oz = 1 quart plus ¼ cup

1 gallon = 128 fl. oz. = 4 quarts

TEMPERATURE

450°F = 230°C = 8 (hot)

425°F = 220°C = 7 (hot)

400°F = 200°C = 6 (moderately hot)

350°F = 180°C = 4 (moderate)

325°F = 165°C = 3 (moderate)

300°F = 150°C = 2 (slow)

250°F = 125°C = ½ (very slow)

225°F = 110°C = ¼ (very slow)

MASS

1 cup olive or vegetable oil, water, wine, vinegar = 236.6 ml (rounded above to 250ml)

½ oz = 14 grams

2 oz = 57 grams

3 oz = 85 grams

4 oz = 113 grams

5 oz = 142 grams

6 oz = 170 grams

8 oz = 227 grams

10 oz = 283 grams

12 oz = 340 grams

16 oz = 454 grams

INDEX

AFRICA

ETHIOPIA

THE SHERATON ADDIS

From the crystal clear pool with soft underwater music to the yearly Ethiopian art exhibition, the hotel is the perfect place to indulge and experience the culture of Addis Ababa.

Taitu Street, P.O. Box 6002
Addis Ababa
telephone 251 11 517 1717
facsimile 251 11 517 2727

theluxurycollection.com/addis

ASIA

CHINA

THE ASTOR HOTEL

Located in the heart of Tianjin, this architectural gem offers guests access to amenities such as a water-based treadmill and a hotel museum. It is also in walking distance to the Xiao Bai Lou, a pedestrian mall that guests can explore.

33 Taier Zhuang Road, Heping District
Tianjin 300040
telephone 86 22 2331 1688
facsimile 86 22 2331 6282

theluxurycollection.com/astor

CHINA

THE CASTLE HOTEL

Overlooking vibrant Xinghai Bay, The Castle Hotel boasts three sophisticated restaurants, a lounge, and a spa. Its grand ballrooms serve as settings for truly memorable occasions.

600 Binhai West Road
Shahekou District
Dalian, Liaoning 116023
telephone 86 411 8656 0000
facsimile 86 411 8656 0056

theluxurycollection.com/castle

CHINA

THE HONGTA HOTEL

Sweeping views of Shanghai, personalized butler service, and the award-winning Italian restaurant Danieli's make one's stay at The Hongta Hotel a first-class experience.

889 Dong Fang Road, Pudong District
Shanghai 200122
telephone 86 21 5050 4567
facsimile 86 21 6875 6789

theluxurycollection.com/hongta

CHINA

THE ROYAL BEGONIA

Exceptional Spanish style, luxury settings, and personalized services combined with indigenous local attractions and culinary arts make this hotel a world-class destination. Our Begonia restaurant features authentic Southeast Asian cuisines complemented with typical Spanish signature dishes.

Haitang Beilu, Haitang Bay, Sanya
Haitang Bay, Hainan 572013
telephone 86 898 3885 9999
facsimile 86 898 3885 7777

theluxurycollection.com/royalbegonia

CHINA

TWELVE AT HENGSHAN

Located on the beautiful tree-lined Hengshan Road, this modern, stylish newcomer is a stone's throw from the city's trendy shopping area, restaurants, parks, and museums.

12 Hengshan Road, Xuhui District
Shanghai 200031
telephone 86 21 3338 3888
facsimile 86 21 3338 3999

luxurycollection.com/12hengshan

INDIA

ITC GARDENIA

Situated in the commercial heart of the city, ITC Gardenia is Asia's first LEED Platinum-rated hotel and embodies the splendors of nature through its wind-cooled lobby and vertical gardens.

No. 1 Residency Road, Bengaluru,
Karnataka 560025
telephone 91 80 2211 9898
facsimile 91 80 2211 9999

theluxurycollection.com/royalgardenia

INDIA

ITC GRAND CENTRAL

Centrally located, the hotel offers stunning views of the city from its rooftop lounge, Point of View. The city's British colonial style is eloquently reflected in the architecture of the hotel.

287, Dr Babasaheb Ambedkar Road,
Parel, Mumbai
Maharashtra 400012
telephone 91 22 2410 1010
facsimile 91 22 2410 1111

theluxurycollection.com/itcgrandcentral

INDIA

ITC GRAND CHOLA

In homage to South India's imperial Cholas, the architecture, ornate design, and ambience of the ITC Grand Chola call upon its grand roots. It features the grandest conferencing facilities in Chennai.

No. 63 Mount Road, Guindy, Chennai
Tamil Nadu 600032
telephone 91 44 2220 0000
facsimile 91 44 2220 0200

theluxurycollection.com/itcgrandchola

INDIA

ITC KAKATIYA

The hotel marks a renaissance in service and style in the commercial and most picturesque part of the city.

63-3-1187, Begumpet, Hyderabad
Andhra Pradesh 500016
telephone 91 40 2340 0132
facsimile 91 40 2340 1045

theluxurycollection.com/itckakatiya

INDIA

ITC MARATHA

Influenced by the Maratha Dynasty and Maharashtrian hospitality, the hotel fuses elegance with history through its thoughtfully designed interior and extensive art collection.

Sahar Airport Road, near International Airport
Andheri (East), Mumbai
Maharashtra 400099
telephone 91 22 2830 3030
facsimile 91 22 2830 3131

theluxurycollection.com/itcmaratha

INDIA

ITC MAURYA

With distinctive architecture inspired by the grand Mauryan Dynasty, this iconic hotel has long been the favored accommodation of heads of state, royalty, celebrities and business leaders from across the world.

Diplomatic Enclave, Sadar Patel Marg,
New Delhi, New Delhi 110021
telephone 91 11 2611 2233
facsimile 91 11 2611 3333

theluxurycollection.com/itcmaurya

INDIA

ITC MUGHAL

Opulent and exquisite, the award-winning ITC Mughal is sprawled over 35 acres of luxurious gardens and located near the Taj Mahal and other historic city sites, such as the Agra Fort and Fatehpur Sikri.

Taj Ganj, Agra
Uttar Pradesh 282001
telephone 91 562 402 1700
facsimile 91 562 233 1730

theluxurycollection.com/itcmughal

INDIA

ITC RAJPUTANA

Located in the heart of town, the hotel offers a host of comforts and services in settings that reflect the spirit of Rajasthan and its royalty.

Palace Road, Jaipur
Rajasthan 302006
telephone 91 141 510 0100
facsimile 91 141 510 2102

theluxurycollection.com/itcrajputana

INDIA

ITC SONAR

Nestled amid acres of land, resplendent with greenery, sunshine, and water, the ITC Sonar is the perfect haven to retreat to and escape from the hustle and bustle of everyday life.

JBS Haldane Avenue (Opp. Science City)
Kolkata, West Bengal 700046
telephone 91 33 2345 4545
facsimile 91 33 2345 4455

theluxurycollection.com/itcsonar

INDIA
ITC WINDSOR

Perfect for business or pleasure, this stately hotel is located steps from the business center of Bangalore and across the way from the Bangalore Golf Course.

Windsor Square, 25, Golf Course Road,
Bangaluru, Karnataka 560052
telephone 91 80 2226 9898
facsimile 91 80 2226 4941

theluxurycollection.com/itcwindsor

INDONESIA
KERATON AT THE PLAZA

This beautiful hotel celebrates the richness of Indonesian culture and local Javanese traditions through its art gallery and cuisine.

Jl. MH. Thamrin Kav. 15
Jakarta 10350
telephone 62 21 5068 0000
facsimile 62 21 5068 9999

theluxurycollection.com/keraton

INDONESIA
THE LAGUNA

Nestled on Bali's finest white-sand beach overlooking the majestic Indian Ocean and infinite swimmable lagoons, The Laguna is situated perfectly in the enchanting Nusa Dua enclave.

Kawasan Pariwisata Nusa Dua Lot N2
Nusa Dua, Bali 80363
telephone 62 361 771327
facsimile 62 361 772163

theluxurycollection.com/bali

MALAYSIA
THE ANDAMAN

Stunning sunsets, crystal blue waters, rainforest trails, and coral reef walks are just some of the extraordinary experiences this hotel offers guests.

Jalan Teluk Datai
Langkawi, 07000
telephone 60 4 959 1088
facsimile 60 4 959 1168

theluxurycollection.com/andaman

THAILAND
THE NAKA ISLAND

With endless views of Phang Nga Bay and the Phuket landscape, this five-star island retreat is private, romantic, and idyllic.

32 Moo 5, Tambol Paklok
Amphur Thalang, Naka Yai Island
Phuket 83110
telephone 66 76 371 400
facsimile 66 76 371 401

theluxurycollection.com/nakaisland

THAILAND
THE SHERATON GRANDE SUKHUMVIT

This hotel is home to Basil, one of the finest Thai restaurants in Bangkok, where chef Kesinee Wanta crafts creative dishes with the exquisite flavors from every culinary region of Thailand.

250 Sukhumvit Road
Bangkok 10110
telephone 66 2 649 8888
facsimile 66 2 649 8000

theluxurycollection.com/grandesukhumvit

THAILAND
VANA BELLE

Poised overlooking the breathtaking Gulf of Siam, Vana Belle offers an enchanting getaway and memorable experiences in one of Thailand's most beautiful locations.

9/99 Moo 3, Chaweng Noi Beach, Surat Thani
Koh Samui 84320
telephone 66 77 915 555
facsimile 66 77 915 556

theluxurycollection.com/vanabellesamui

EUROPE

AUSTRIA
HOTEL BRISTOL

Located near the Vienna State Opera in the heart of the city, this luxury hotel provides an oasis from the bustle of a busy metropolis.

Kaerntner Ring 1
Vienna 1010
telephone 43 1 515 160
facsimile 43 1 515 16550

theluxurycollection.com/bristol

AUSTRIA
HOTEL GOLDENER HIRSCH

Sip the signature Susanne cocktail, eat the famous Rigo Jancsi dessert, and live in luxury while attending nearby summer festivals in Salzburg.

Getreidegasse 37
Salzburg 5020
telephone 43 6 628 0840
facsimile 43 6 628 43349

theluxurycollection.com/goldenerhirsch

AUSTRIA
HOTEL IMPERIAL

Transport back to nineteenth-century Vienna by enjoying a cup of specially brewed Imperial tea and a slice of the renowned torte at this elegant and beautiful hotel.

Kaerntner Ring 16
Vienna, 1015
telephone 43 1 501 100
facsimile 43 1 501 10410

theluxurycollection.com/imperial

AUSTRIA
SCHLOSS FUSCHL

Enjoy a valuable collection of Old Masters, a lush golf course, and fresh fish from the castle fishery at this hotel.

Schloss Strasse 19
Hof bei Salzburg 5322
telephone 43 6 229 22530
facsimile 43 6 229 2253 1531

theluxurycollection.com/schlossfuschl

BULGARIA
SOFIA HOTEL BALKAN

Located in downtown Sofia, this luxury hotel offers an exceptional experience of Bulgaria's finest culture and service.

5 Sveta Nedelya Square
Sofia 1000
telephone 359 2 981 6541
facsimile 359 2 980 6464

theluxurycollection.com/sofia

FINLAND
HOTEL KÄMP

Guests have the opportunity to visit the world-famous Kämp Bar and Brasserie Kämp during their stay at this beautiful hotel.

Pohjoisesplanadi 29
Helsinki 00100
telephone 358 9 576 111
facsimile 358 9 576 1122

theluxurycollection.com/kamp

FRANCE
PRINCE DE GALLES

Just steps away from the Champs-Élysées, this Art Deco hotel, a mosaic of discrete Parisian elegance, is located in the heart of the city and offers exceptional hospitality and superbe cuisine by culinary talent Stéphanie Le Quellec

33 Avenue George V
Paris 75008
telephone 33 1 53 237777
facsimile 33 1 53 237878

theluxurycollection.com/princedegalles

GERMANY
HOTEL ELEPHANT

Fine dining, cooking lessons with Michelin-starred chef Marcello Fabbri, and guided cultural tours are all offered at this unique hotel.

Markt 19
Weimar 99423
telephone 49 3643 8020
facsimile 49 3643 802610

theluxurycollection.com/elephant

GERMANY
HOTEL FUERSTENHOF

Relax in the AquaMarin spa, the landscaped pool, the Finnish sauna, or the Roman steam bath and restore harmony to your body at this luxury hotel.

Troendlinring 8
Leipzig 04105
telephone 49 341 1400
facsimile 49 341 1403700

theluxurycollection.com/fuerstenhof

GREECE
MYSTIQUE

Guests can visit the Secret Wine Cave, take in the beauty of the surrounding views, and restore at the spa while visiting this luxury resort.

Oia
Santorini Island
Santorini, South Aegean 84702
telephone 30 228 607 1114
facsimile 30 228 607 1115

theluxurycollection.com/mystique

ITALY
HOTEL DANIELI

Located within walking distance of Saint Mark's Square, this legendary hotel allows visitors to shop, dine, and experience Venice to the fullest.

Castello 4196
Venice 30122
telephone 39 041 522 6480
facsimile 39 041 520 0208

theluxurycollection.com/danieli

GREECE
ARION RESORT & SPA

A private beach, captivating sea views, and a concierge who can arrange a magnificent expedition to the Temple of Poseidon are all here for guests at this unique resort.

40 Apollonos Street–Astir Palace Complex
Athens-Vouliagmeni 16671
telephone 30 210 890 2000
facsimile 30 210 896 2583

theluxurycollection.com/arion

GREECE
THE ROMANOS

Enjoy special bath amenities at Anazoe Spa, tours from Navarino Outdoors, and scuba diving with Navarino Sea—all experiences guests can have at this spot.

Navarino Dunes, Messinia
Costa Navarino 24001
telephone 30 272 309 6000
facsimile 30 272 309 6500

theluxurycollection.com/theromanos

ITALY
HOTEL EXCELSIOR

The Neapolitans' love of excellent food can be experienced in this hotel's restaurants, including the La Terrazza roof garden restaurant.

Via Partenope 48
Naples 80121
telephone 39 081 764 0111
facsimile 39 081 764 9743

theluxurycollection.com/excelsiornaples

GREECE
BLUE PALACE

Discover beauty in this hotel's emblematic views, tranquillity at its Elounda Spa on the beach, and fun at the nearby Crete Golf Club.

P.O. Box 38
Elounda, Crete 72053
telephone 30 284 106 5500
facsimile 30 284 108 9712

theluxurycollection.com/bluepalace

GREECE
SANTA MARINA

A paradise within a paradise, this hotel is a tranquil oasis where one can indulge in spa treatments and fine dining surrounded by the natural beauty of Mykonos.

Ornos Bay
Mykonos, South Aegean 84600
telephone 30 228 902 3220
facsimile 30 228 902 3412

theluxurycollection.com/santamarina

ITALY
HOTEL PITRIZZA

Experience local traditions and cuisine firsthand with the hotel's full immersion opportunities, including local artisan demonstrations.

Costa Smeralda
Porto Cervo 07020
telephone 39 0789 930111
facsimile 39 0789 930611

theluxurycollection.com/hotelpitrizza

GREECE
KING GEORGE

Just two kilometers from the Acropolis, this hotel has welcomed many celebrities and hosted many events in its 350-square-meter room under the illuminated sky.

Vas Georgiou A' Street 3
Athens 10564
telephone 30 210 322 2210
facsimile 30 210 322 8034

theluxurycollection.com/kinggeorge

GREECE
VEDEMA

Surrounded by historical sites, beautiful beaches, and hot springs, this luxury resort has plenty to explore.

Megalohori
Santorini, South Aegean 84700
telephone 30 228 608 1796
facsimile 30 228 608 1798

theluxurycollection.com/vedema

ITALY
HOTEL ROMAZZINO

Enjoy local food and activities such as horse riding and sailing at this beautiful resort.

Costa Smeralda
Porto Cervo 07020
telephone 39 0789 977111
facsimile 39 0789 977614

theluxurycollection.com/romazzino

GREECE
HOTEL GRANDE BRETAGNE

With unsurpassed views of the Acropolis and Parthenon, Constitution Square, and Lycabettus Hill, this hotel offers unrivaled access to Athens's mythical history.

Constitution Square
Athens 105 64
telephone 30 210 333 0000
facsimile 30 210 322 8034

theluxurycollection.com/grandebretagne

ITALY
HOTEL CALA DI VOLPE

Horse riding, tennis, and golf are just some of the fun outdoor activities to enjoy at this hotel.

Costa Smeralda
Porto Cervo 07020
telephone 39 0789 976111
facsimile 39 0789 976617

theluxurycollection.com/caladivolpe

ITALY
THE GRITTI PALACE

Occupying a prestigious setting on the Grand Canal, The Gritti Palace was reopened in 2013 after a meticulous restoration. A leisurely short stroll from Piazza San Marco, the imposing palazzo awards rare views of Santa Maria della Salute.

Campo Santa Maria del Giglio
Venice 30124
telephone 39 0417 94611
facsimile 39 0412 5200942

theluxurycollection.com/grittipalace

THE NETHERLANDS
HOTEL DES INDES

This luxury hotel is located in the heart of
The Hague and is an ideal starting point
for exploring local attractions such as the
Royal Picture Gallery Mauritshuis and the
antique market.

Lange Voorhout 54-56
The Hague 2514 EG
telephone 31 70 361 2345
facsimile 31 70 361 2350

theluxurycollection.com/desindes

RUSSIA
HOTEL NATIONAL

Exploring Moscow was never easier, as
this hotel offers spectacular views of the
Kremlin and Red Square, while being only
steps away from attractions such as the
Bolshoi Theatre.

15/1 Mokhovaya Street
Moscow 125009
telephone 7 495 258 7000
facsimile 7 495 258 7100

theluxurycollection.com/national

SPAIN
HOTEL MARQUÉS
DE RISCAL

Frank Gehry's design houses a collection
of wines that any wine lover will enjoy. The
hotel offers guided cultural tours to truly
take in the surrounding area.

Calle Torrea 1
Elciego 01340
telephone 34 945 180880
facsimile 34 945 180881

theluxurycollection.com/marquesderiscal

THE NETHERLANDS
HOTEL PULITZER

Unique tours, such as the boat tour, the
concierge tour, and the gardens tour are
offered at this luxury hotel.

Prinsengracht 315-331
Amsterdam 1016 GZ
telephone 31 20 5235235
facsimile 31 20 6276753

theluxurycollection.com/pulitzer

SERBIA
METROPOL PALACE

This hotel has always been the heart of
Belgrade's social life and is an indelible
landmark in the city skyline, overlooking
Tasmajdan Park.

Bulevar Kralja Aleksandra 69
Belgrade 11000
telephone 381 11 333 3100
facsimile 381 11 333 3300

theluxurycollection.com/metropolpalace

SWITZERLAND
HOTEL PRESIDENT
WILSON

Located minutes away from Geneva's
lakefront, this luxury hotel allows one to
explore such local attractions as the Jet d'Eau,
Flower Clock, and St. Peter's Cathedral.

47, Quai Wilson
Geneva 1211
telephone 41 22 906 6666
facsimile 41 22 906 6667

theluxurycollection.com/presidentwilson

POLAND
HOTEL BRISTOL

This hotel lies right on the Royal Route, a
road that leads through the historic district
of the city and is dotted with examples of
stunning architecture from the sixteenth
century to the present day.

Krakowskie Przedmiescie 42/44
Warsaw 00-325
telephone 48 22 551 1000
facsimile 48 22 625 2577

theluxurycollection.com/bristolwarsaw

SPAIN
HOTEL ALFONSO XIII

This hotel is one of the most monumental
landmarks in Seville, embodying the city's
layered history, architecture, and authentic
cuisine in a luxurious atmosphere.

San Fernando 2
Seville 41004
telephone 34 95 491 7000
facsimile 34 95 491 7099

theluxurycollection.com/hotelalfonso

TURKEY
LUGAL

Immerse yourself in local culture, as
original paintings by local artists are
found throughout this luxury hotel.

Noktali Sokak No. 1, Kavaklidere
Ankara 06700
telephone 90 312 457 6050
facsimile 90 312 457 6150

theluxurycollection.com/lugal

PORTUGAL
CONVENTO DO
ESPINHEIRO

Enjoy wine-tasting sessions, bread-
baking classes, Alentejo folk-singing
performances, and Gregorian chants at
this luxury resort.

Convento do Espinheiro
Évora 7000
telephone 351 266 788200
facsimile 351 266 788229

theluxurycollection.com/convento

SPAIN
CASTILLO HOTEL SON VIDA

A first-class beauty spa, breathtaking golf
courses, and a Kids' Club equipped with a
separate pool area and playground are all
offered at this hotel.

C/Raixa 2, Urbanizacion Son Vida
Mallorca 07013
telephone 34 971 493493
facsimile 34 971 493494

theluxurycollection.com/castillo

UNITED KINGDOM
THE PARK TOWER
KNIGHTSBRIDGE

Dine at the patriotic Grenadier Pub, visit the
vibrant Serpentine Gallery, and sip London's
most expensive and glamorous cocktail, the
Diamond Martini, while at this hotel.

101 Knightsbridge
London, England SW1X 7RN
telephone 44 207 235 8050
facsimile 44 207 235 8231

theluxurycollection.com/parktowerlondon

PORTUGAL
THE SHERATON ALGARVE/
PINE CLIFFS RESIDENCE

Enjoy breathtaking views of the
surroundings, warm weather year-round,
and beautiful golf course, including its
famed and most challenging golf hole
Devil's Parlour, at this luxury hotel.

Praia de Falesia, Apartado P.O. Box 644
Albufeira 8200
telephone 351 289 500100
facsimile 351 289 501950

theluxurycollection.com/algarve
theluxurycollection.com/pinecliffs

SPAIN
HOTEL MARIA CRISTINA

Indulge in a mouthwatering local culinary
experience when visiting this charming
hotel, near the Michelin-starred restaurants
of San Sebastián.

Paseo Republica Argentina 4
San Sebastián 20004
telephone 34 943 437600
facsimile 34 943 437676

theluxurycollection.com/mariacristina

UNITED KINGDOM
TURNBERRY

Site of the famous "Duel in the Sun" by
Jack Nicklaus and Tom Watson, this hotel
is an outdoorsman's sanctuary, with quad
biking, horseback riding, and off-roading
offered.

Turnberry Ayrshire KA26 9LT
Scotland
telephone 44 165 533 1000
facsimile 44 165 533 1706

theluxurycollection.com/turnberry

UKRAINE
HOTEL BRISTOL

Located directly in the city center, this hotel has had more than a century of notable guests and is just steps from museums and venues for opera, ballet, and orchestral performances.

Pushkinskaya Street, 15
Odessa 65026
telephone 380 48 796 5500
facsimile 380 48 769 5503

theluxurycollection.com/bristolodessa

LATIN AMERICA

ARGENTINA
PARK TOWER

Unparalleled service, an in-hotel shopping arcade, and a heart-of-the-city location set this luxury hotel apart.

Avenida Leandro N. Alem 1193
Buenos Aires 1001
telephone 54 11 4318 9100
facsimile 54 11 4318 9150

theluxurycollection.com/parktower

CHILE
SAN CRISTOBAL TOWER

A bicycle tour of the bohemian Bellavista neighborhood, picnics at the nearby Concha y Toro Vineyard, and skiing on the best slopes in South America are all offered at this luxury hotel.

Josefina Edwards de Ferrari 0100
Santiago
telephone 56 2 2707 1000
facsimile 56 2 2707 1010

theluxurycollection.com/sancristobaltower

CHILE
VILLARRICA PARK LAKE

Enjoy breathtaking views while climbing one of the most active volcanoes in South America. Experience thrills while bungee jumping, and relax in nearby hot springs while at this hotel.

Camino Villarrica—Pucon Km 13
Villarrica
telephone 56 45 45 00 00
facsimile 56 45 45 02 02

theluxurycollection.com/villarrica

MEXICO
HACIENDA PUERTA CAMPECHE

This hotel is a collection of restored seventeenth-century historical houses, allowing one to enjoy the beauty of a Mexican hacienda with excellent personal service.

Calle 59, No. 71 por 16 & 18
Campeche, Campeche 24000
telephone 52 981 816 7508
facsimile 52 981 816 7375

theluxurycollection.com/
puertacampeche

MEXICO
HACIENDA SAN JOSE

An authentic Mayan experience can be had in the Mayan Villas, while luxury can be found through massages in the privacy of the spa area.

KM 30 Carretera Tixkokob-Tekanto
Tixkokob, Yucatán 97470
telephone 52 999 924 1333
facsimile 52 999 924 1534

theluxurycollection.com/sanjose

MEXICO
HACIENDA SANTA ROSA

Bird watching, Mayan lessons, cocktail demonstrations, and tours of the botanical garden are all offered at this luxury hotel.

KM 129 Carretera Merida Campeche
Santa Rosa, Yucatán 97800
telephone 52 999 923 1923
facsimile 52 999 923 1653

theluxurycollection.com/santarosa

MEXICO
HACIENDA TEMOZON

Explore the unique Hol Be Spa, where one can experience individual spa treatments in a beautifully preserved cavern.

KM 182 Carretera Merida-Uxmal
Temozon Sur, Yucatán 97825
telephone 52 999 923 8089
facsimile 52 999 923 7961

theluxurycollection.com/temozon

MEXICO
HACIENDA UAYAMON

Bulbous pegs set into stone walls can be found throughout this hotel, allowing guests to hang woven cotton hammocks and sleep in the Mayan style.

KM 20 Carretera Uayamon-China-Edzna
Uayamon, Campeche
telephone 52 981 813 0530
facsimile 52 999 923 7963

theluxurycollection.com/uayamon

PERU
HOTEL PARACAS

A bottle of local pisco, wind-surfing lessons, and private-jet flights over the Nazca Lines are all offered at this luxury hotel.

Av. Paracas S/N
Paracas
telephone 51 56 581 333
facsimile 51 56 581 501

theluxurycollection.com/hotelparacas

PERU
PALACIO DEL INKA

Located in the historic center of Cusco, this hotel dates back almost five centuries and offers easy access to museums, markets, and restaurants. Its property also boasts a relaxing therapy pool.

Plazoleta Santo Domingo 259
Cusco
telephone 51 84 231 961
facsimile 51 84 233 152

theluxurycollection.com/palaciodelinka

PERU
TAMBO DEL INKA

Enjoy views of the Vilcanota River while swimming in the hotel pool. Take a guided trip to the Valle Sagrado and escape to Machu Picchu from the hotel's private train station.

Avenida Ferrocarril S/N
Sacred Valley, Urubamba
telephone 51 84 581 777
facsimile 51 84 581 778

theluxurycollection.com/tambodelinka

THE MIDDLE EAST

KUWAIT
THE SHERATON KUWAIT

Situated in the middle of Kuwait's commercial center, the hotel boasts a health club that offers a variety of revitalizing, relaxing, and pampering treatments.

Safat 13060 / Fahd Al-Salem Street
P.O. Box 5902 Safat
Kuwait City 13060
telephone 965 2242 2055
facsimile 965 2244 8032/4

theluxurycollection.com/kuwait

U.A.E.
AJMAN SARAY

Situated along the Arabian Gulf, just minutes from Dubai, our resort overlooks endless expanses of pristine sand and sparkling water.

Sheikh Humaid Bin Rashid Al Nuaimi Street
Ajman 8833
telephone 971 6 714 2222
facsimile 971 6 714 2223

theluxurycollection.com/ajmansaray

U.A.E.
AL MAHA

Arabian wildlife—with Arabian oryx and gazelles as the star attractions—can be seen from the temperature-controlled infinity pools or sundeck areas of all villas.

Dubai—Al Ain Road
Dubai
telephone 971 4 832 9900
facsimile 971 4 832 9211

theluxurycollection.com/almaha

U.A.E.
GROSVENOR HOUSE

The first hotel to be launched in Dubai Marina, this is a prominent lifestyle destination in a cosmopolitan area, with a wide range of fantastic restaurants and bars.

Al Sofouh Road
P.O. Box 118500
Dubai
telephone 971 4 399 8888
facsimile 971 4 317 6980

theluxurycollection.com/grosvenorhouse

NORTH AMERICA
UNITED STATES
THE BALLANTYNE

Located on a championship PGA golf course, this Southern beauty features signature cocktails, luxurious lodging, and spa treatments.

10000 Ballantyne Commons Parkway
Charlotte, North Carolina 28277
telephone 704 248 4000
facsimile 704 248 4005

theluxurycollection.com/ballantyne

UNITED STATES
THE CANYON SUITES AT THE PHOENICIAN

Guests of the Canyon Suites enjoy complimentary daily wine tastings, chauffeured resort and local transportation, as well as a private infinity pool.

6000 East Camelback Road
Scottsdale, Arizona 85251
telephone 480 941 8200
facsimile 480 423 2881

theluxurycollection.com/canyonsuites

UNITED STATES
THE CHATWAL

This Stanford White landmark was once home to the famed Lambs Club and now offers guests the same glamorous treatment with luxurious accommodations and striking Art Deco interior design.

130 West 44th Street
New York, New York 10036
telephone 212 764 6200
facsimile 212 764 6222

theluxurycollection.com/chatwal

UNITED STATES
THE EQUINOX

With beautiful mountain views, horse-drawn wagon rides, and suites with fireplaces, enjoy cozy days and nights at this Vermont treasure.

3567 Main Street
Manchester Village, Vermont 05254
telephone 802 362 4700
facsimile 802 362 4861

theluxurycollection.com/equinox

UNITED STATES
THE FAIRFAX AT EMBASSY ROW

Located in the center of Washington, D.C., this hotel serves high diplomatic guests and offers luxurious dining at its new restaurant, 2100 Prime.

2100 Massachusetts Avenue
Northwest Washington, D.C. 20008
telephone 202 293 2100
facsimile 202 293 0641

theluxurycollection.com/fairfax

UNITED STATES
HOTEL IVY

The Hotel Ivy is a luxurious spa destination in Minneapolis that hosts the Ivy Spa Club and connects guests by climate-controlled skyway to attractions such as the Orchestra Hall and world-class shopping.

201 South Eleventh Street
Minneapolis, Minnesota 55403
telephone 612 746 4600
facsimile 612 746 4890

theluxurycollection.com/ivy

UNITED STATES
THE LIBERTY

Guests of the beautiful hotel are exposed to the best of Boston, from sweeping views of the skyline to complimentary Liberty-branded bicycles for riding around town.

215 Charles Street
Boston, Massachusetts 02114
telephone 617 224 4000
facsimile 617 224 4001

theluxurycollection.com/libertyhotel

UNITED STATES
THE NINES

Known for its creative and unique personal service, this hotel offers guests a customized nightly turn-down, and a seasonal and tasty snack.

525 SW Morrison Street
Portland, Oregon 97204
telephone 877 229 9995
facsimile 503 222 9997

theluxurycollection.com/thenines

UNITED STATES
PALACE HOTEL

Commanding its location in the heart of vibrant San Francisco, this hotel provides guests with hospitality on a grand scale.

2 New Montgomery Street
San Francisco, California 94105
telephone 415 512 1111
facsimile 415 543 0671

theluxurycollection.com/palacehotel

UNITED STATES
THE PHOENICIAN

Golfing, swimming, tennis, and first-class spa treatments are some of the activities guests can enjoy at this awe-inspiring Sonoran destination.

6000 East Camelback Road
Scottsdale, Arizona 85251
telephone 480 941 8200
facsimile 480 947 4311

theluxurycollection.com/phoenician

UNITED STATES
THE ROYAL HAWAIIAN

Experience Hawaiian hospitality to its fullest, with views of the Diamond Head Crater and the hotel's brand-new signature drink, the Smokin' Mai Tai, at this ultra-luxe "Pink Palace."

2259 Kalakaua Avenue
Honolulu, Hawaii 96815
telephone 808 923 7311
facsimile 808 931 7098

theluxurycollection.com/royalhawaiian

UNITED STATES
SLS HOTEL AT BEVERLY HILLS

Designed by Philippe Starck, the hotel challenges every traditional convention of luxury hospitality, from a culinary program crafted by Spanish chef José Andrés to a unique spa concept at Ciel Spa.

465 S. La Cienega Boulevard
Los Angeles, California 90048
telephone 310 247 0400
facsimile 310 247 0315

theluxurycollection.com/sls

UNITED STATES
THE ST. ANTHONY

Located in the heart of historic San Antonio, and in walking distance of the famed River Walk, this national landmark hotel features first-class amenities including the Peacock Alley Bar, where guests can enjoy a cocktail in the plush leather chairs next to the fireplace.
Opening Summer 2014.

300 East Travis Street
San Antonio, Texas 78205
telephone 210 227 4392

theluxurycollection.com

UNITED STATES
THE US GRANT

A presidential landmark nestled amid the vibrancy of downtown San Diego's famed Gaslamp Quarter, the hotel weaves its storied history into an oasis of fine art and epicurean innovation—including The US Grant's 100-day barrel-aged Centennial Manhattan.

326 Broadway
San Diego, California 92101
telephone 619 232 3121
facsimile 619 232 3626

theluxurycollection.com/usgrant

JOSHUA DAVID STEIN writes about food, travel, fashion, and style for publications like *Esquire, The New York Times, T: The New York Times Style magazine, New York magazine, Food & Wine, The Guardian, Wired,* and *Vice,* for whom he writes food-based erotica. He is currently the restaurant critic for *The New York Observer* and was formerly the senior editor of *Departures* magazine, the editor of *Black Ink,* and the editor-in-chief of *BlackBook* magazine. He is the co-author of *StyleCity: New York* (Thames & Hudson, 2009). He lives with his wife, Ana, and two children, Achilles and Augustus, in the Morningside Heights section of New York City.